M000098958

LEARNABLE
MOMENTS
for Moms

---

100 DEVOTIONS TO DISCOVER
GOD IN THE EVERYDAY

Erin Greneaux

ISBN: Erin Greneaux

ISBN-13: 978-0-692-04129-1

All scriptures marked NIV and from the Holy Bible, New International Version®, NIV®, Copyright © 1973, 1978, 1984, 2011 by Biblica, Inc®.

Dedication

To my daughters, Maya and Everly.
You are an incredible blessing to my life!
May God bless you and keep you as you grow up in the knowledge
of him, and may you follow him all of the days of your lives.

Table of Contents

Acknowledgements

Thank you to the many people who helped make this book a reality! Ann Yeager, thank you for the countless hours that you spent editing this manuscript. Adriane Tiel, thank you for your creative attention to detail and design in creating the cover. Jane Heels, thank you for the beautiful picture you took of my girls for the cover, and for dealing with all of the crying and tantrums that occurred in the process. Mom and Dad, thank you for making sure that the devotional applications had a correct and Biblically-based theological perspective.

Nathan, thank you for not only dealing with frozen dinners, piles of laundry, and a generally messy house while I worked on this project, but also for encouraging me every step of the way to pour out my heart in these pages. Finally, thank you to my girls, who gave me grace during this season and shared my time and attention with this project. I have discovered that ironically, the biggest obstacles to my writing a book on motherhood are the ones who call me mom!

Introduction

Dear fellow mothers,

This devotional was written in the middle of so many nights, after waking up to feed the baby and not being able to go back to sleep in spite of absolute exhaustion because these words were burning inside me. On so many days, I waited patiently for my kids to overlap even a little bit of nap time so that I could pull out my computer and put to paper the many lessons that God was revealing to me as a mom of these precious littles. I hope that these words meet you right where you are.

I know you, dear reader, because I am you! I understand the struggle of loving being a mom and yet desiring something more. I feel the lack of sleep and mommy brain that makes me wonder if I will ever think like a rational person again. I understand the struggle of my quiet time with God becoming reduced to a broken record of praying for the baby to please, please, please just go to sleep. I too wonder if laundry, diaper changes, and feedings are all that God has left for me to do for his kingdom.

I hope these daily devotions speak to you in this unique season of life, because here is the truth, friends; God is not finished with you! Not only is he using you in the eternal work of raising children with hearts that long after him, but he also has another season around the corner that will be just as unique and fulfilling as this one is. You are still capable of thinking deep thoughts, overcoming spiritual challenges, and seeing God reveal himself to you even in the midst of a cluttered sea of brightly-colored toys. I am convinced that each season of life prepares us for the season that is to come, so let's make use of this time by preparing our hearts and minds through a deeply personal and consistently growing relationship with Christ.

Over the next one hundred days, you are going to become intimately acquainted with my two precious daughters. Maya is two and a half, and everything that comes with that. She is imaginative, smart, energetic, talkative, full of life, and so much fun! She is also independent, strong-willed, persistent, and challenging. I wouldn't change a thing about her, but I'm glad that her sister is different, because I can only keep up with one Maya. Everly, eight months old, is Maya's opposite in every way. She is full of joy, content, snuggly, and easy-going. She takes whatever life gives her with a smile. She lights up every room.

Each day I will share a real-life, unedited, and unexaggerated story from my girls' lives. I will then give a scripture that the experience made me think of and how I personally used that situation to connect to God in a way that challenged me, encouraged me, or taught me something new about his character. Rather than teachable moments, which we always look for with our kids, these are learnable moments. They answer the question, "How can I grow in my relationship with God in this unique season?"

My hope is that once you see how these learnable moments have come up in my life as a mom, you will be able to identify your own learnable moments and create a habit of personal spiritual growth on a daily basis through your everyday experiences. Each devotion ends with a prayer and a question for personal reflection. I encourage you to write out your answers so that you can hold yourself accountable to apply what you have learned in a practical way.

I hope these one hundred days leave you feeling refreshed, deeply rooted in the Word, more in touch with God's daily work in your life, and more equipped to continue growing ever closer to the lover of your soul!

Sincerely,

Erin Greneaux

I Try Again

Maya is very determined, and I love that she always wants to "try again." However, in true toddler style, she sometimes demonstrates this trait to a fault. The other day she was running down the sidewalk, when she tripped and scraped her knee. It was the kind of scrape that makes me cringe as a mom because I can almost feel the grating of sidewalk on skin just by watching.

She burst into tears. I picked her up and put her on my lap as she held out her palms and knees for me to examine. One knee was bleeding, but she would be fine.

"Do you want to get in the stroller so I can take you home?"

"No!" she wailed, crying even louder, "I have to try again!" She stood up, tears streaming down her face, blood trickling down her knee. She wiped her nose with the back of her hand and started running again. I couldn't have been more proud of her!

Read

Do you not know that in a race all the runners run, but only one gets the prize. Run in such a way as to get the prize. Everyone who competes in the games goes into strict training. They do it to get a crown that will not last, but we do it to get a crown that will last forever. Therefore I do not run like someone running aimlessly; so that after I have preached to others, I myself will not be disqualified for the prize.

—1 Corinthians 9:24–26a, 27b NIV

Apply As moms, we do a lot of running around, and it can be tempting to think that what we do doesn't matter in the grand scheme of things. Changing diapers, feeding kids, and cleaning the same clothes, dishes, and messes over and over again can seem menial. However, the truth is that we are doing courageous work, and the race we are running has eternal consequences. We are shaping the hearts and minds of our children, and the first picture of God that they see is the one that we portray to them.

Not only is what we do important, but even more so the way in which we do it. The perspective, attitude, and motivation that we carry is contagious to the children watching us. As we run this race, we must make sure to take time with God each day so that our minds will stay on eternal things rather than the temporary. And when we fall down, we have to get back up and try again!

Pray Father, give me the diligence and perseverance to run my race well today. Help me to remember that I have a mandate with eternal consequences to set an example of Christ for my children in everything that I do, even the daily, repetitive tasks.

Reflect How can I change my attitude toward a certain task this week?

Day Two

Sitting Up

At four months old, Everly, started sitting up. Once this happened, over a one-week period everything changed. All she wanted to do was sit up. If there was anything that used a reclining position, she wanted nothing to do with it.

The swing was replaced with a jumperoo. A box of toys on the rug took the place of the activity gym with its hanging toys. The boppy seat was chosen in favor of the bouncer. For naps we had to move her from the bassinet to her crib. Even trying to clip her into her reclining car seat was a struggle. Once Everly discovered the advantages of sitting up, it was a whole new world, and she wasn't going back.

Read

When I was a child, I talked like a child, I thought like a child, I reasoned like a child. When I became a man, I put the ways of childhood behind me. For now we see only a reflection as in a mirror; then we shall see face to face. Now I know in part; then I shall know fully, even as I am fully known. And now these three remain: faith, hope and love. But the greatest of these is love.

—1 Corinthians 13:11–13 NIV

Apply Everly's graduation from laying down to sitting up is a lot like our transformation into Christ-likeness. Once we surrender our lives to Christ and experience his perspective, it is like seeing the world sitting up for the first time. Everything looks different, and we realize what a narrow and skewed view we had before. All of the excuses, strategies, and games that we used in order to get our way seem childish as we embrace a life that is focused on love. Once we taste this genuine freedom, there is no turning back.

The best part is that there is even more freedom to be experienced in the future. I know that there is more for Everly—one day she will graduate from sitting to walking, and her horizons will broaden once again. In the same way, we only see and understand God's love in part while we are in this life, like the image reflected in a mirror. How wonderful will be the day when we see God face to face and experience his love in full!

Pray Father, thank you for your love for me that changes the way I view myself and the world. I eagerly look forward to the day when I fully know you in the way that you fully know me!

Reflect In what ways have I put childish habits behind?

_____

_____

_____

Day Three

I No Want That

"Mommy, I can have some green beans?" Maya asked one night as I was fixing the plates for dinner. This didn't surprise me. Maya loves her vegetables, especially green beans.

"You want some green beans?" I asked.

"Yes," she confirmed.

"Okay, I'll get you some." I put the plates on the table and went back to the refrigerator to take out the green beans. I came back to the table and put a few on her plate. The whole process took twenty seconds, but it was long enough for Maya to change her mind.

"No! I no want green beans!" Sometimes dealing with a toddler can make me question my sanity.

"What? You just asked me for green beans, and I got you some. Now you don't want them?"

"No! Get it off my plate!" I sighed, taking back the green beans. Meal times with toddlers. Help me, Jesus! Maya may be fickle, but I relate with her far too often!

Read So I say to you: Ask and it will be given to you; seek and you will find; knock and the door will be opened. Which of you fathers, if your son asks for a fish, will give him a snake instead? Or if he asks for an egg, will give him a scorpion? If you then, though you are evil, know how to give good gifts to your children, how much more will your father in heaven give the Holy Spirit to those who ask him!

—Luke 11:9–13 NIV

Apply Sometimes it is difficult to trust God because he gives us challenges that we didn't ask for. Other times he gives us exactly what we ask for and we suddenly change our minds, realizing that it wasn't what we wanted after all. Sometimes he gives us a blessing so incredible that we aren't sure how to handle it! Thankfully, no matter what we ask God for or think we want, he knows just what we need and will always provide it.

In the same way that we as parents want to provide for our children, God delights in giving to us. Know that God has good gifts in store for us! They may not be the ones that we have imagined for ourselves, but they are the right gifts, and God's timing with those gifts is perfect.

Pray Father, thank you for knowing what I need even before I know it. Thank you for promising to provide for my needs and for going even further by giving me so many blessings. Help me to trust your plan and your timing as I wait for the things that I ask for.

Reflect What is one unexpected gift from God that I can thank Him for?

Day Four

I Too Busy Right Now

On a Sunday morning when Maya was eighteen months old, we had finally finished getting everyone ready for church and were heading out the door.

"Okay, Maya. It's time for church, let's go get in the car," I directed. She wasn't in the middle of a project at the time, just circling around and around the coffee table.

She considered me for a moment and said, "No, I too busy right now," and went back to circling. My first reaction was to think, "What? You're one and a half—what could possibly be keeping you busy?" My second reaction was a realization that she was using a line that she had heard me say over and over again.

Read *Let us hold unswervingly to the hope we profess, for he who promised is faithful. And let us consider how we may spur one another on toward love and good deeds, not giving up meeting together, as some are in the habit of doing, but encouraging one another--and all the more as you see the Day approaching.*

—Hebrews 10:23–25 NIV

Apply   Even though the challenges and tasks in our lives seem like big deals to us, in the grand scheme of things, they are all small. While we are busy being busy with them, God is reaching out, waiting for us to spend time with him and to invest in eternal pursuits. We have to actively be on guard against being too busy to love God and love others. This verse is a great reminder of the importance of not only spending quality time with God, but also of spending time with other believers, sharing what we have learned and encouraging one another in the faith. We must keep in mind that activities are temporary, but relationships are eternal. We must intentionally invest in experiences of corporate worship, Bible study, and service.

Pray   Father, help me to value the eternal by making a priority of spending time with other Christians, encouraging and being encouraged in the faith. Show me ways that I can share what you are teaching me with others, and give me the courage and discipline to follow through in obedience.

Reflect   Who do I need to meet with to encourage today?

_____

_____

_____

_____

_____

Day Five

Can You Spot The Snacks?

Maya was in rare form the day we took the baby bump pictures for my pregnancy with Everly. She was running away, crying, and breaking photo props. It was terrible. I was sure there wouldn't be a usable picture in the entire session. We eventually pulled out some animal crackers to lure Maya over like one would a dog with a treat. We would hide an animal cracker in the place where we wanted her to be in the picture, get everyone else set up, and then wait for her to come find it while the photographer snapped some candid shots.

Any pictures with even a hint of a smile from her only had to do with food. We finally decided to call it quits when she dumped the whole bag of animal crackers into the fountain. Miraculously, our photographer was able to get a few good ones which we posted on our personal social media pages for friends and family to see. When people gushed about how great our pictures turned out, I couldn't help but laugh and tell them to try to find the animal crackers hiding in every photo.

Read   *You shall not covet your neighbor's house. You shall not covet your neighbor's wife, or his male or female servant, his ox or his donkey, or anything that belongs to your neighbor.*   —Exodus 20:17 NIV

18

Apply   It can be tempting to look at family pictures on social media and wonder why our families aren't quite as polished and serene as the smiling faces of our friends'. Social media makes it easy to think that every other family has it all together. Instead of believing that we are the only ones who have struggles, we must recognize that every family has their own version of "animal crackers" and chaos behind the scenes.

We seem to do well being content with our house and our family until we see someone else's. Whether it is seeing a picture-perfect kitchen on Pinterest or a renovated mudroom on Instagram, we are quick to imagine how much better our lives would be if we had the same. God warns us in the ten commandments to stay far away from the comparison trap. We can only experience joy in his blessings and the freedom that comes with contentment when we stop comparing the family photos. The truth is that none of these images represent reality.

Pray   Father, I'm sorry for the ways in which I have not shown gratitude for the blessings you have given me and for envying the house, family, or life of someone else. Help me to find contentment in the circumstances and season that I am experiencing right now!

Reflect   What am I tempted to envy about others' families?

_____

_____

Day Six

All You Want

One of Maya's favorite activities is moving a group of things from one place to another. One day she was moving her crayons from one room to another, one handful at a time, and had instructed me to stay in the room where she was moving them. She brought me a coloring book and then spent the next twenty minutes excitedly running back and forth between the two rooms, bringing me more and more crayons from her big crayon bucket.

The whole time she was showering me with crayons, she was saying in the happiest voice, "All you want, Mommy! I get all you want! Here is more! All you want!"

She was getting so much joy out of sharing her crayons with me, and the feeling was contagious.

Read

Consider this: Whoever sows sparingly will also reap sparingly, and whoever sows generously will also reap generously. Each one should give what he has decided in his heart to give, not out of regret or compulsion. For God loves a cheerful giver. And God is able to make all grace abound to you, so that in all things, at all times, having all that you need, you will abound in every good work. As it is written: "He has scattered abroad His gifts to the poor; His righteousness endures forever."

—2 Corinthians 9:6–9 NIV

Apply In a culture where we live surrounded by a mentality of scarcity, we need to remember that we serve a God who created everything and has no limitations or confinements. Not only does God not need anything from us, there is nothing that we could ask of him that he isn't capable of fulfilling. His desire is to lavish these gifts on us, promising not only material provision, but also a calling to serve him and a sense of purpose and fulfillment in that work.

Even more, Christ is eternal life to us—he is all we want! These promises do come with a precursor though, which is a heart of generosity towards others that finds joy in giving. Cheerful generosity is so much easier to achieve when coupled with God's promise of provision, is it not?

Pray Father, allow me to give generously and cheerfully to those in need around me. Allow me to trust your promise of provision in my life so that I hold back nothing from those you call me to love through time, service, or material possessions.

Reflect What is one need I can ask God to fill? What is one need that I can fill for someone else?

_____

_____

_____

_____

_____

Day Seven

What You Doing in This World?

I have come to expect the unexpected to come out of Maya's mouth, but the other day she said something that literally stopped me in my tracks.

Out of the blue, she asked, "Mommy, what you doing in this world?" I was stunned. How very existential of my two year old! It took me a second to realize that she must have heard someone say, "What in the world are you doing?" and this was her translation. Nevertheless, the question, so central to humanity, so blunt and straightforward, had me stop and ask myself—what am I doing in this world? I was suddenly glad that she wasn't actually trying to ask that question, because I was at a loss of how to answer.

Read   *If I speak in the tongues of men and of angels, but do not have love, I am only a resounding gong or a clanging cymbal. If I have the gift of prophecy and can fathom all mysteries and all knowledge, and if I have a faith that can move mountains, but do not have love, I am nothing. If I give all I possess to the poor and give over my body to hardship that I may boast, but do not have love, I am nothing.*

—1 Corinthians 13:1–3 NIV

Apply There are a lot of things we can do in the world, but in the end, all that matters is love. It is not the what, but the why, the motivation behind it, that will remain. So the real question is not, "what are you doing in this world?" but rather, "why are you doing it?" There are many reasons why we do the things that we do—to gain power, to earn love, to feel worthy, to achieve prestige, to cover a hurt, to calm a fear, or to redeem a wrong.

If we want the true motivation for our actions to be to love others, then we must have something else taking care of all of the needs listed above. The only way that we can act in love is to embrace the Father's love for us, allowing it to fill us up, heal us, care for us, and restore us. When our fulfillment is complete in his love, we have all the resources we need to love others wholly and completely, and we can focus on being rather than doing.

Pray Father, show me how to love others today. Show me any areas where I am doing the right things for the wrong reasons. Give me the discernment to know when I have allowed the action I'm taking to become more important than the reason for taking it. Thank you for your love which fulfills all my needs.

Reflect In what ways am I focused on what I am doing rather than who I am being?

_____

_____

_____

_____

Day Eight

Eating Playdough

Maya loves to play with playdough. She has a set where she can make playdough hair grow on a plastic person, then she can style it or cut it. We have two rules with the playdough—keep it off of the carpet, and don't eat it. She really wants to eat it. It doesn't help that most playdough sets are food related, which is why we ended up with the hair one.

Every now and then, the urge to eat the playdough becomes too great. Maya isn't very sneaky, though. She will get a piece and say, "I going to check on something, Mommy. Stay here. Not come too." She will then run from the room and usually go hide in my closet, where I will find her sitting on the floor between the hanging clothes and putting playdough in her mouth. Thankfully, playdough is non-toxic, although it is difficult to get out of her teeth. I am always sad when playdough time takes this turn because it means we have to put the playdough away, and the fun is over.

Read

Where can I go from your Spirit? Where can I flee from your presence? If I go up to the heavens, you are there; if I make my bed in the depths, you are there. If I rise on the wings of the dawn, if I settle on the far side of the sea, even there your hand will guide me, your right hand will hold me fast. If I say, "Surely the darkness will hide me and the light become night around me," even the darkness will not be dark to you; the night will shine like the day, for darkness is as light to you.

—*Psalm 139:7–12 NIV*

Apply   While it is wonderful to know that God never leaves us, we sometimes have the urge to tell God to stay away for a little while, especially when we are doing something that we know is against the boundaries he has set in his Word. Even if we think we have hidden something from him in a dark secret corner of our lives, he knows it. We don't get to pick and choose when to have God around. If God is comfort in our loneliness, he is also conviction in our sinfulness. If he is peace when things are out of our control, he is also the perfection that reveals how we come up short. While it may seem like an invasion of privacy, God's true motivation is to bring us close to him by constantly encouraging us to become more like Christ. Let's allow his light to shine on the dark places of our lives so that they can be light too!

Pray   Father, thank you for your constant presence and that you never leave or forsake me. Please help me to see the areas where I need to become more like Christ, and give me the courage to bring them to light so that I can experience the freedom that comes from obedience.

Reflect   What is one way that I can become more like Christ?

God is Great, God is Good

    Maya recently started going to Mother's Day Out one day a week so that I can run some errands with just one little girl instead of two. It is wonderful! One of the things that I like about it is that she has a chance to learn some new things that I haven't taught her. I have been teaching her to pray, but not any memorized prayers. One day, she came home from "school," and I could tell that she had been learning the typical pre-meal prayer for kids.

    I smiled to myself as I could hear her in the back seat reciting in her sweet little voice, "God is great...God is good...." Ah, what a joy it is to be a mom of a child whose heart is seeking after the Lord! She continued, "God is drinking some tea...God is reading a book... God is Jesus...," (*Yes! She gets it!*) "God is a puppy dog...," (*No, definitely not.*) Her list continued for some time with a very creative rendition of God being and doing lots of things that I'm pretty sure he isn't, but it was funny nonetheless.

Read   *Then the Lord came down in the cloud and stood there with him and proclaimed his name, the Lord. And he passed in front of Moses, proclaiming, "The Lord, the Lord, the compassionate and gracious God, slow to anger, abounding in love and faithfulness, maintaining love to thousands, and forgiving wickedness, rebellion and sin. Yet he does not leave the guilty unpunished; he punishes the children and their children for the sin of the parents to the third and fourth generation."*

—*Exodus 34:5–7 NIV*

Apply It is easy to have an inaccurate view of God based on who we want him to be in the moment. If we want to get away with something, he is a God of grace. If we have been slighted, he is a God of justice. Sometimes we see him as too distant and holy to approach, while other times we treat him with far too much familiarity. The fact is that God is a being perfectly balancing so many seemingly opposing characteristics that he is difficult for our human minds to grasp.

Thankfully, the Bible gives us many pictures of who God is-— unchanging (Mal. 3:6), all-knowing (Is. 46:9-10), all-powerful (Job 11:7-11), everywhere (Jer. 23:23-24), wise (Rom. 11:33), faithful (2 Tim. 2:13), good (Ps. 34:8), just (Deut. 23:4), merciful (Rom. 9:15-16), gracious (Ps. 145:8), love (John 4:7-8), holy (Rev. 4:8), and the list could go on for a long time. In order to follow God, we must trust him, and in order to trust him, we must truly know who he is.

Pray Dear Father, help me to know you. Show me who you truly are and not simply who I want you to be for me in each moment. Give me the courage to trust you for who I have seen you to be in the Bible and in my own life.

Reflect In what ways have I viewed God in a manner that is inconsistent with his character?

Day Ten

It's a Tunnel

We had an unfortunate event in which Maya fell off of a counter head first onto the tile floor in the kitchen. Yes, my child and I have survived every mother's nightmare. Everly was only three weeks old at the time, and I didn't want my newborn anywhere near the emergency room of the hospital. So my husband took Maya into the hospital while Everly and I waited in the car (trying pretty unsuccessfully to remain calm). My husband called me throughout the process to give me updates.

When he told me that they were going to do a CT scan to check for any brain damage or skull fractures, I immediately started worrying about how Maya would do during the test. I could picture her going inside the dark tube filled with loud noises and being strapped down so that she would stay still. The whole process sounded like a traumatic disaster waiting to happen. Nathan called me again as soon as it was over, and I frantically asked about how she had responded.

"She was completely fine!" he said to my relief, "When she saw it, she said, 'Look, Daddy, a tunnel!'" Thank goodness she loves tunnels. But honestly, I think her resilience in the situation came from the fact that her Daddy was with her.

Read

The Lord is my shepherd, I lack nothing. He makes me lie down in green pastures, he leads me beside quiet waters, he refreshes my soul. He guides me along the right paths for his name's sake. Even though I walk through the darkest valley, I will fear no evil, for you are with me; your rod and your staff, they comfort me.

—Psalm 23:1–4 NIV

Apply

These well-known verses don't say "even though I might walk through a somewhat low-light valley," they say "though I walk through the darkest valley." There will be times in life when we walk through the darkest valleys of loss, pain, rejection, fear, and loneliness. The dark valleys are a guarantee in life. However, we have another guarantee that gives us peace and hope in the valleys—the Lord is with us in the midst of it.

Being in God's presence doesn't change the circumstances, but it does change our perspective in the midst of them. Instead of seeing the impossible, we see our God, with whom nothing is impossible. Instead of seeing death, we see Christ, who is our eternal life. Instead of being overcome, we experience the Holy Spirit, who gives peace that passes understanding. Even scary moments can seem like another adventure when our "Daddy" is near!

Pray

Father, thank you for the promise that you are with me in the difficult seasons of life. I pray for your perspective when the circumstances seem overwhelming.

Reflect

How has God changed my perspective in the midst of a valley in my life?

29

Day Eleven

This a Pizza

Maya is just starting to really use her imagination to pretend and make believe, which is such a fun season! We were playing outside in the backyard where I had given her some old pans and utensils to use for "cooking." She found some big, wild mushrooms growing under a tree. I quickly told her that she could play with them but not eat them because they could be dangerous. I could understand the appeal—the tops were at least three inches across, they had a spongy texture, and the underside had layers of white lines that would fold over when touched. To a two year old, they were absolutely mystifying.

She pulled off all of the mushroom tops and laid them out flat in her dish. After sprinkling on various other pieces of nature (flower petals, leaves, dirt, etc.), she proudly brought the dish over to me. Holding it out, she said, "You want to eat one, Mommy?"

"Not for real," I reminded her.

"No, just pretend," she replied, "This a pizza!"

"Oh, it looks delicious," I said, pretending to eat it.

Read

Woe to those who call evil good and good evil, who put darkness for light and light for darkness, who put bitter for sweet and sweet for bitter.

—Isaiah 5:20 NIV

Apply In the culture we live in, it is easy to lose sight of right and wrong. The world takes something that we know is dangerous, it dresses it up so that it isn't quite as recognizable, and it lets us play with it and see its appeal. The world even tells us that it is something else, something good. Soon, we have forgotten the danger, and it becomes so familiar that we take a bite and experience the unpleasant consequences.

As parents, we know that rules exist for our children's good and safety. The rules aren't random or placed to control or frustrate. However, we sometimes believe that God places boundaries in our lives to keep us from having any fun. The only way to steer clear of these lies and continue to see light and dark for what they truly are is to stay in constant communication with God. We must rely on him to reveal to us right from wrong and to convict us when we start sliding in the wrong direction.

Pray Father, show me how I have slipped into darkness so that I can change that way of thinking and behaving. Thank you for your laws, given for my protection.

Reflect What is one sin in my life that I have excused or rationalized rather than confronted?

_____

_____

_____

_____

Day
Twelve

Stain Remover

I don't know if all children are as messy as Maya when it comes to eating, but she leaves a disaster behind after every meal. I'm not even sure how she gets food in the places that she does. A simple snack of carrot sticks and hummus somehow turns into smashed chickpeas on her face, in her hair, on her arms, legs, and feet, all over her clothes, and even in her diaper. If we are eating spaghetti, I simply plan on giving her a bath after because I know that any other type of cleaning up is going to be pointless.

The stain remover I use on her clothes should really give me a discount to buy in bulk because we go through bottles of the stuff. No matter how many times I clean Maya up, she is only one meal away from becoming a hopeless mess all over again. To make matters worse, Maya absolutely detests it when I try to wipe her face and hands. It is a constant battle. While she doesn't like feeling sticky, she hates the process of being cleaned up even more.

Read   *Cleanse me with hyssop, and I will be clean: wash me, and I will be whiter than snow. Let me hear joy and gladness; let the bones you have crushed rejoice. Hide your face from my sins and blot out all my iniquity.*

—Psalm 52:7–9 NIV

Apply We are constantly in need of cleaning as well. We have the promise of forgiveness because Jesus paid for our sins on the cross. When we surrender our lives to Christ, God forgives all of our sins—past, present, and future. We are clean! However, being clean is not the same thing as staying clean. While we are always forgiven, we will still struggle daily with sin. We still need to make a habit of coming before God to confess our mistakes and ask forgiveness for specific sins that he convicts us for.

Sometimes, no matter how much we want to be clean, we are unwilling to face the sins that we are covered in. We don't want to do the tough work of changing those habits, thoughts, and attitudes so that we don't live in those messy patterns any more. One day, I hope that Maya will master using a fork, and then she won't have as many messes for me to clean. It is the same way with us. While forgiveness makes us clean, we have to do the difficult work of changing how we live in order to keep from returning to the same filth over and over again.

Pray Father, thank you for the promise of forgiveness for all of my sins. Help me to actively take on the difficult task of identifying harmful, sinful practices in my life and learning how to change them so that I don't remain in a damaging cycle of sin.

Reflect What is one thought pattern, attitude, or action I need to change in order to break a habit of sin in my life?

Day Thirteen

Starting the Day Off Right

I am convinced that toddlers naturally have multiple personalities. I can usually tell what kind of day we are going to have based solely on how Maya wakes up in the morning.

Sometimes she wakes up with an agenda already in mind, saying, "Mommy, I want to work a puzzle!" Other days she wakes up crying, either sad or scared. Occasionally, she starts out sassy, saying, "Mommy, where aaaare you?" My favorite is when she wakes up quiet and cuddly, wanting to just sit in my lap in silence for a few minutes before saying anything. Pretty frequently she wakes up with food on the brain (a girl after my own heart), "Mommy, we having waffles for breakfast?" I wonder if Maya knows what kind of day she will have based on how I greet her in the morning?

Read

'When one rules over people in righteousness, when he rules in the fear of God, he is like the light of morning at sunrise on a cloudless morning, like the brightness after rain that brings grass from the earth.' "If my house were not right with God, surely he would not have made with me an everlasting covenant, arranged and secured in every part; surely he would not bring to fruition my salvation and grant me my every desire.'"

—2 Samuel 23:3b–5 NIV

Apply David writes these verses after God promises to have his descendant rule on the throne forever (through Jesus). He is overcome with how God has blessed his family. He knows that following God's rules when it comes to leading a family results in an environment filled with joy. I think I speak for most moms when I say that we rarely feel like the "brightness after rain" when we get up in the mornings. Depending on how many hours of sleep we get and how many times we are woken up, we can usually better represent the storm itself.

If we can focus on Christ and depend on his strength to get through the many struggles each day, large and small, then we can have the joy that only comes from him infiltrating our lives and pouring out to our children. We too have been given an everlasting covenant of salvation that we pass on from generation to generation. Our eternal life in Christ is secure, and we can celebrate that with our children!

Pray Father, please give me a contagious joy today in spite of the challenges that I will face. Help me to lead my children in righteousness so that I will not simply trudge through another day, but shine like the morning at sunrise!

Reflect How can I lead in righteousness today?

_____

_____

_____

Day Fourteen

Kissing Baby Jesus

This past Christmas, we started telling Maya the Christmas story from the Bible. We talked about baby Jesus and how we are celebrating his birth. We got her a little wooden nativity scene to play with and used the characters to act out the story countless times. When we would go for walks around the neighborhood looking at the lights, I would always point out the nativity scenes. I wasn't really sure how much she was taking in at age one and a half, but I figured it was worth talking about either way.

One day we walked on a new street and came across a house with a big nativity scene in the front yard. It had all of the characters, all lit up, at least three feet tall, and bigger than Maya. She stopped on the sidewalk and just stared at them all. When she started to walk towards them, I beckoned her back to the sidewalk.

But she said, "I kiss baby Jees." I wasn't about to stop her. She walked right up to the manger in the middle with the little baby Jesus in it. She carefully bent over and kissed him right on the forehead and then patted his belly gently with her hand. For a moment, it was as if the whole world stood still and held its breath. I can only imagine the feeling of awe at that first Christmas.

Read

So [the shepherds] hurried off and found Mary and Joseph, and the baby, who was lying in the manger. When they had seen him, they spread the word concerning what had been told them about this child, and all who heard it were amazed at what the shepherds said to them. But Mary treasured up all these things and pondered them in her heart. The shepherds returned, glorifying and praising God for all the things they had heard and seen, which were just as they had been told.

—Luke 2:16–20 NIV

Apply

We have heard the Christmas story so many times, but seeing it through a child's eyes can be magical. A child's reaction to this amazing event can definitely help us experience the story anew. What an incredible gift God gave us as his Son was born into the world to give us life. Like Mary, we should take some time to treasure the full magnitude of this event and ponder it in our hearts.

I love how the shepherds, "when they had seen him," went and told everyone they could the good news! Let us take some time today to truly see Jesus so that we can have the same infectious desire to share the good news with those around us.

Pray

Father, thank you for sending your Son, God himself, into the world as a vulnerable baby to experience all of the confinements of humanity. Thank you for the incredible gift that you gave me on that first Christmas!

Reflect

How can I treasure this story in my heart today?

Day Fifteen

Sharing My Toys

When an only child like Maya suddenly becomes a sister at the ultra-emotional age of two, there are bound to be some struggles. For Maya, deciding to share her time with Mommy, as well as sharing her toys, were part of that learning curve. Sometimes, I would be so impressed with how generous she was, and other days it was not so pretty.

For the first several months of Everly's life, when she could only spend time laying down, Maya would constantly bring her little offerings to keep her happy. If I left the room and came back, I never knew what I would find beside her. Maya would accessorize her with a hat, tuck her in with a blanket, befriend her with a stuffed animal, or bury her under a mountain of toys. One day I found a shoe box that Maya had placed next to Everly. When I picked it up, it was heavy. I opened it to find that Maya had packed all kinds of treasures for her sister—important things like a ball, a guitar pick, a sippy cup, a hairbrush, etc. I hope that Maya's generous spirit continues into adulthood. More importantly, I hope that it rubs off on me!

Read

One person gives freely, yet gains even more; another withholds unduly, but comes to poverty. A generous person will prosper; whoever refreshes others will be refreshed.—Proverbs 11:24–25 NIV

Apply Of course, we all know that giving is more important than getting and that it feels good to give to others. However, as moms, we sometimes feel like we should be exempt from giving to others because we give and give and give to our children! This verse reminds us of the truth that when we are generous, we will be refreshed.

I love this idea of refreshing others and being refreshed! It shows a perfect picture of how generosity is so much more than giving things or writing tax-deductible checks, but can truly be a lifestyle. Refreshing others can take the form of an encouraging word, a smile, grace extended rather than condemnation, a listening ear, or a patient and empathetic response. These are things that we can give to everyone that we come into contact with. They leave a wake of refreshment in our lives and the lives of those around us. When we choose to give these intangible gifts, we gain even more!

Pray Father, thank you for the many ways that you refresh me day to day. Use me to refresh others around me in the same way. Forgive me for the times that I withhold from others the hope and life that you have given me.

Reflect What can I give freely today?

_____

_____

_____

_____

Day Sixteen

Just Come to Me

Maya wanted to go outside to swing, but her timing was not the best. It had been threatening to rain all day, and right as we stepped outside, it started to sprinkle lightly.

"Maya, it's starting to rain. Let's wait until after it rains, and then we can go swing on the swing," I tried to persuade her, standing under the covered back porch.

"No, Mommy, I want to swing! Not worry, I just run." She ran almost all the way to the swings and stopped short when she realized that I was still standing under the porch.

"I don't want to get wet," I told her, "But you can play until it starts raining harder."

She beckoned to me with both hands, trying to coax me over as you would a scared dog. "It's okay, Mommy, just run to me!" I just stood there. "Just run to me, Mommy, run to me!" she continued trying to persuade me. "It's okay if you run!" She finally won me over, and I ran to her. I pushed her on the swing until the shower blew over.

Read

[Jesus speaking] "No one can come to me unless the Father who sent me draws them, and I will raise them up at the last

day. It is written in the Prophets: 'They will all be taught by God.' Everyone who has heard the Father and learned from him comes to me. No one has seen the Father except the one who is from God; only he has seen the Father. Very truly I tell you, the one who believes has eternal life.

—John 6:44–47 NIV

Apply This world is full of darkness and death. Without Christ, we are lost with no hope. However, Jesus makes it clear in these verses that separation from God is not his plan for us. Instead, we can be saved and have eternal life by believing in him. Sometimes we view God as hiding, being aloof and mysterious, making it difficult for us to find him.

These verses show that his intentions are the exact opposite. The words Jesus says are a perfect picture of him standing in the rain, beckoning us to run to him. He does not want any to be lost in the storm of sin in this life, but is drawing the lost to himself so that we might be saved. Once we run to him and experience that safety, how could we not help join him in the task of beckoning those around us?

Pray Father, thank you for drawing me to yourself, seeking me out, and calling me to run to Jesus for salvation. Thank you for giving me the incredible gift of eternal life and forgiveness of sins through Jesus. Help me not to fear the darkness of this world, knowing that I will be with you in heaven one day.

Reflect How can I participate in the work of beckoning others to Christ?

Day Seventeen

You Can Do It

While I was at the end of my pregnancy with Everly, everyday activities with an active toddler began to get more and more difficult. Sitting on the floor to play was a feat, trying to read a book with Maya on my lap was comical, and playing on a child-sized playground with her was simply exhausting.

One day, she was playing in her little tent. "Mommy, come in!" she called to me. I could barely fit in her tent without being eight months pregnant.

"I'm too big to fit in your tent right now, but I can poke my head in," I offered. She was not satisfied. Then she did what we all love and hate as parents—she quoted me back to myself.

"You can do it, Mommy, just try!" she said with optimistic encouragement. I love that she is learning perseverance, but I would rather not have that same perseverance applied to me. After a lot of groaning, wiggling, and scooting, I successfully crammed myself into the little tent, bent over under the short roof, my knees touching Maya's in the tight space. Maya had the biggest smile, "Good job, Mommy! You did it!" Of course I had known that it was physically possible for me to fit in the tent, I just hadn't wanted to go through the work it would take to accomplish it.

Read

I have learned to be content whatever the circumstances. I know what it is to be in need, and I know what it is to have plenty. I have learned the secret of being content in any and every situation, whether well fed or hungry, whether living in plenty or in want. I can do all things through him who gives me strength.

—*Philippians 4:11b–14 NIV*

Apply

While the last verse is well-known, we rarely look at it within the context of the verses that come before it. We know that we can do all things through Christ, but there are a lot of things that we don't want to do or are simply unwilling to do. If we claim this verse and use it to accomplish great things that we never dreamed that we could achieve, then we shouldn't be surprised when God whispers it back to us when he calls us to do menial, ordinary, or even demeaning tasks for him.

Doing all things means just that—all things. Living the Christian life is not easy. It is messy. God wants us to say "yes, I can do it" to whatever he calls us to—big or small, easy or difficult, glamorous or monotonous. Whatever our circumstances, contentment comes when we say "yes" even when it means making a sacrifice.

Pray

Father, thank you for laying out good plans for me. Forgive me for the times that I agree only to the plans that I want to be a part of, rather than all that you have called me to do.

Reflect

What do I need to say "yes, I can do it" to today?

Day
Eighteen

One More Time

Maya is strong-willed. While she is not the most strong-willed child in the world, she is definitely not the most compliant one I've ever met either. As a child, I needed only a disapproving look from one of my parents before dissolving into remorse. Maya requires much more than that! Raising her up in the way that she should go is a tedious task that requires careful consistency in consequences for actions, clear communication of boundaries, and repeating these first two steps over and over and over and over.

I read in a parenting book that I only have to hold the boundary and consequence one more time than she tests it. It is literally a battle to see which of us can outlast the other. While this bit of knowledge was meant to be encouraging, it is really just exhausting. I won't lie—some days she wins. This process is no fun, and it reminds me of a similar one that we experience as adults.

Read

Then Peter came to Jesus and asked, "Lord, how many times shall I forgive my brother or sister who sins against me? Up to seven times?"

Jesus answered, "I tell you, not seven times, but seventy-seven times.

—Matthew 18:21–22 NIV

"Then the master called the servant in. 'You wicked servant,' he said, 'I canceled all that debt of yours because you begged me to. Shouldn't you have had mercy on your fellow servant just as I had on you?'

—*Matthew 18:32–33 NIV*

Apply Forgiveness is a tedious job of setting boundaries, watching those boundaries be broken again and again, and continuing to extend forgiveness time after time. The process is not fun, and it is not easy, but we have the strength to complete it and outlast any who come against us. How do we have such a wealth of forgiveness in us? Because we have been forgiven much! God literally moved heaven and earth to send his Son, Jesus, to take our sins by paying the price that we deserved to pay for the things that we have done wrong. He continually forgives all that we do, say, and think that goes against the boundaries that he has set for us, so we must be faithful in forgiving others. Only when we focus on Christ's forgiveness extended to us do we have the ability to extend it to others.

Pray Father, thank you for the forgiveness that you give me through Christ's sacrifice on the cross. I do not take it for granted! Please give me the strength to do the difficult work of persevering in forgiveness for those who hurt me.

Reflect Who do I need to forgive (again) today?

_____

_____

Day Nineteen

Watch This

I'm pretty sure Maya is the messiest eater in the world. I try really hard to encourage her to use utensils rather than her fingers and also discourage just putting her face in the plate. One day we were having yogurt for snack. I pretty much plan on needing to change her clothes after yogurt. I gave her the bowl of yogurt with a spoon and a bib the size of Texas that I knew would do little good.

"Remember to take small bites so that it doesn't get everywhere, ok?" I instructed. She started off doing really well. Her hair was in a ponytail, so at least it would stay clean, and she was doing a great job with her spoon. My hopes for a clean getaway began to grow. I turned to spoon some baby food to Everly. When I looked back at Maya she had the bowl in both hands holding it up to her face, trying to lick the yogurt out with her tongue like a dog.

"Maya," I warned, "If you don't use your spoon, I'm taking the yogurt away." She looked at me, considering her options.

"Watch this, Mommy," she said putting the bowl down on the table. She picked up her spoon, scooped up a giant mound of yogurt, and licked it off the spoon like a dog, slopping it all over the front of her clothes. "I use my spoon!" she smiled defiantly. I sighed. Where does she learn this stuff?

Read

Be careful, however, that the exercise of your rights does not become a stumbling block to the weak. For if someone with a weak conscience sees you, with all your knowledge, eating in an idol's temple, won't that person be emboldened to eat what is sacrificed to idols? So this weak brother or sister, for whom Christ died, is destroyed by your knowledge. When you sin against them in this way and wound their weak conscience, you sin against Christ. Therefore, if what I eat causes my brother or sister to fall into sin, I will never eat meat again, so that I will not cause them to fall.

—Corinthians 8:9–13 NIV

Apply

As Christians, we have been given freedom in Christ. Sometimes, we like to take this freedom to the extreme. While we follow what God says, we try to find any gray area that isn't specifically identified and take advantage of it. While this may not hurt our conscience as we follow Christ, Paul admonishes us in these verses to think of others. Christians who are not as mature in their faith may find such loose obedience as a stumbling block in their own lives. This is especially true when children are around to watch. They not only notice these small inconsistencies, but they also master them surprisingly quickly.

Pray

Father, help me represent whole-hearted obedience to my fellow Christians and to my children. Show me any areas where my freedom causes others to question their faith.

Reflect

In what area do I practice loose obedience, and how does that attitude affect others?

Day Twenty

The Elephant in the Room

Everly has a pacifier with a stuffed animal elephant attached to it that she loves. One day, the elephant suddenly went missing. It was on the bouncer one minute and gone the next. When things disappear in this way, Maya is usually the culprit. She has a love of organizing things around the house by putting them where she thinks they should go, rather than where they belong.

I asked if she had seen Everly's elephant, and she replied vaguely, "I not see it."

"I don't see it either," I replied, "But do you know where it is?" She walked away pretending like she hadn't heard me. A few days of these conversations went by with Maya offering no help. One night after putting Maya to bed, I searched all of her usual hiding places and discovered a new one. A flap of fabric in the back of the recliner can hold things like a pocket. It had the elephant, a guitar pick, a ball, a bag clip, and some hair ties. Jackpot!

The next morning I told Maya I found the elephant, "Do you know where I found it?" She shook her head.

I showed her the spot, "Did you know it was there?" She nodded. "Everly needed it. You didn't want to get it for her?"

"No," she said simply.

Read   *This is how we know what love is: Jesus Christ laid down his life for us. And we ought to lay down our lives for our brothers and sisters. If anyone has material possessions and sees a brother or sister in need but has no pity on them, how can the love of God be in that person? Dear children, let us not love with words or speech but with actions and in truth. This is how we know that we belong to the truth and how we set our hearts at rest in his presence: If our hearts condemn us, we know that God is greater than our hearts, and he knows everything.*

—*1 John 3:16–20 NIV*

Apply   Maya had become calloused to her sister's needs, and the same happens to us. Who are the people in our lives who are needy for our time, emotions, or stuff who we have become calloused to? Do we see someone in need right in front of us and simply overlook it because we are unwilling to get involved? We may be holding the elephant pacifier that they need to give them comfort, and yet we walk right by pretending that we don't see their need.

Pray   Father, convict my heart when I fail to love those you have placed in my life. Allow me to see the needs around me, and give me the intentional generosity to meet those needs in the way that you have equipped me to. Thank you for providing for me so that I can show love by providing for others.

Reflect   Who do I need to love today, and how?

_____

_____

Acorns

In the fall, Maya went through a squirrel phase. I was pregnant with Everly at the time and trying to walk as much as possible. Every day, Maya and I would take a walk, but we would only get as far as the big oak tree four houses down. The oak tree was right next to the sidewalk and dropped all of its acorns right on the concrete where Maya could see them. Once we got to that spot, Maya would start collecting the smooth, round acorns that fascinated her. Sometimes, she would bring a cup or bucket from home. Other times, she would fill her hands, then my hands, and then my pockets. Once she had collected for the better part of half an hour, and anything that could hold acorns was overflowing, she and I would walk back home with her treasures.

On the walk home, I would try to discreetly drop as many of the acorns as possible. Once we got home, Maya would hide them all around the house like a squirrel. While cleaning later, I would find small clusters here and there. Some would be in her play teapot or in her sock drawer. Occasionally, I would find the huge collection, perhaps in the bottom of the laundry basket. I threw away as many of her stockpiles as I could find, but there is one problem with acorns. They are full of little bugs that eat them up over time. By the time I discovered some of her piles, there were only little pieces left!

Read Do not store up for yourselves treasures on earth, where moth and rust destroy, and where thieves break in and steal. But store up for yourselves treasures in heaven, where moth and rust do not destroy, and where thieves do not break in and steal. For where your treasure is, there your heart will be also.

—Matthew 6:19–21 NIV

Apply The things that we spend so much time and energy gathering in this life are ridiculously temporary. We try to collect things of value, things that will last, but all of these things are passing away before our very eyes. Anything tangible in this life that we work for will wither, pass away, or be left behind. Only two things are eternal and will remain at the end—God and people. We need to be sure that our time, energy, attention, and resources invest in the eternal rather than the temporary. There are a lot of distractions around us, trying to pull our hearts after the treasure that litters this life. We must fight to keep our hearts and our eyes on Christ!

Pray Father, I am sorry for the temporary things in this life that I chase after. Give me a heart that yearns after the eternal, and give me the strength to set aside all that is temporary in pursuit of it!

Reflect What treasure is my heart attached to unnecessarily?

No Diaper

I know that as a mom of young kids, I am understandably tired. If I could describe sleep in one word during this season it would be "interrupted." However, every now and then something happens that makes me realize just how sleep-deprived I really am. One morning after breakfast, Maya was playing, and her pajama shorts caught on a toy and started to pull down. Rather than exposing her diaper, I noticed that she had nothing on under her pajama shorts.

"Maya, are you wearing a diaper?" I asked confused.

"No," she answered simply. What? My mind started reeling. Did I forget to put one on her last night before bed? Had she taken it off by herself in her crib? Was the bed wet? I checked her pajamas—dry. I checked the bed—dry, and there was no diaper in sight. Realization sunk in—the night before I must have put her to bed with pajamas but no diaper! This was not a potty-trained child! How she made it all night without an accident was beyond me, but I was grateful nonetheless. Of all the details to forget in a day, this is one to not let slip. I had sent a toddler to bed for the whole night without any protection against an accident.

Read   *Above all else, guard your heart, for everything you do flows from it. Keep your mouth free of perversity; keep corrupt talk far from your lips. Let your eyes look straight ahead; fix your gaze directly before you. Give careful thought to the paths for your feet and be steadfast in all your ways. Do not turn to the right or the left; keep your foot from evil.*

—Proverbs 4:23–27 NIV

Apply   Sometimes in the repetitive tasks of the day-to-day we forget to do some of the most important things. Small things that make a big difference tend to be the first to go when we grow lax in our walk with Christ. If there is one detail we should not forget in the Christian life, it is the heart. All of our thoughts, words, and actions come from the heart. It is the core that determines obedience or disobedience in our everyday lives. As we get ready for the day, we wouldn't dream of leaving the house without brushing our teeth or putting on deodorant (the bare essentials for even an exhausted mom). Yet we tend to neglect the heart, which, though unseen, is vital to our responsibilities for the day. Taking a few moments to put our hearts in order is essential if we want to avoid having an accident.

Pray   Father, you know my heart and the struggles that continually vie for control. Give me your discernment as I go out today. Show me the paths that I should walk, the words to say, and the thoughts to allow myself to dwell on. Help me guard my heart so that only your love flows from it.

Reflect   How do I need to guard my heart today?

Day Twenty Three

Catch Me

Maya loves to play chase, except she calls it "catch me." She loves to chase Nathan around the house, and she loves for him to chase her. While either one of these makes me a little nervous because of the whole running in the house thing, I try to look the other way for the Daddy-daughter bonding to take place.

Inevitably, a game of "catch me" almost always ends in the same way. Maya is giggling and running, and as Nathan purposely slows down, she pats him with her tiny hand triumphantly.

She turns to run the other direction away from him saying, "Catch me, Daddy!" Instead of looking ahead where she is running, she turns to look back at Nathan to see if he is coming after her. A few more paces and she either trips over a toy or runs into a piece of furniture. And then the usual ensues—crying, cradling, kissing the spot, etc. Eventually she will learn to keep her eyes looking ahead.

Read

Therefore, since we are surrounded by such a great cloud of witnesses, let us throw off everything that hinders and the sin that so easily entangles. And let us run with perseverance the race marked out for us, fixing our eyes on Jesus, the pioneer and perfecter of faith. For the joy set before him he endured the cross, scorning its shame, and sat down at the right

hand of the throne of God. Consider him who endured such opposition from
sinners, so that you will not grow weary and lose heart.

—Hebrew 12:1–3 NIV

Apply As we run our race in life, there are a lot of things that we can focus on. We can look behind us at the past hurts, mistakes, and disappointments. Fixing our eyes on the past will only cause another fall. We can look down at ourselves and see the hardship of a current struggle. Focusing on our current problems will only make us weary and cause us to lose heart. Instead, we should fix our eyes on Christ. He is the one who has a plan for our lives and is leading us to it. He perfects us along the way and equips us with all that we need. By keeping our focus ahead on him, we see Jesus' example in the way that he responded to the struggles and hardships in his life, which he endured for our sake. Then we can be encouraged to keep running our race with optimism.

Pray Father, thank you for the example of Christ, who left heaven to be like me, to experience my struggles, and then to conquer the power of sin in my life. Allow me to keep my focus on his example and to not lose heart.

Reflect In what situation do I need to fix my eyes on Christ today?

_____

_____

_____

_____

Climbing in the Crib

I am one blessed mom. As much as Maya loves to climb, and is very talented at it, she has never tried to climb out of her crib at night or during nap time. (As I write these words, I am tempted to knock on wood.) She does climb into her crib by herself, though. Crazy, right? She will climb into it to get a stuffed animal or her blanket and then ask me to help her get back out. I know that she is physically capable of getting out by herself, she just hasn't ever tried. I hope this lasts forever.

Read

It is for freedom that Christ has set us free. Stand firm, then, and do not let yourselves be burdened again by a yoke of slavery. Mark my words! I, Paul, tell you that if you let yourselves be circumcised, Christ will be of no value to you at all. Again I declare to every man who lets himself be circumcised that he is obligated to obey the whole law. You who are trying to be justified by the law have been alienated from Christ; you have fallen away from grace. For through the Spirit we eagerly await by faith the righteousness for which we hope. For in Christ Jesus neither circumcision nor uncircumcision has any value. The only thing that counts is faith expressing itself through love.

—Galatians 5:1–6 NIV

Apply The believers were arguing over whether circumcision should be a requirement to become a follower of Christ. While this may seem like a trivial argument today, it was a major controversy at the time. We can't point any fingers, though. We have our own unwritten amendments to the Bible's requirements for following Christ. While we know that we are saved by grace through faith in Jesus, we sometimes unconsciously add an "and" to that statement. It could be anything, such as how to dress, eat, worship, or educate. We tend to create a lot of rules for ourselves and others that Christ has set us free from.

In the same way that Maya returns to the bars of her crib, we don't waste any time trying to go back to earning through works the freedom that we could never earn on our own. It is for freedom that we have been set free. Only if we can accept the fullness of God's grace in our own lives will we be able to extend that grace to others.

Pray Father, I am sorry for the ways that I have amended your grace by believing that I must somehow work for your gift of life. Allow me to fully embrace the freedom you offer through Christ, so that I can in turn love those around me more fully.

Reflect What unwritten rules do I need to be free from today?

_____

_____

_____

_____

Day Twenty Five

There are Peacocks out There

Maya's favorite animal is a peacock. I realize this isn't the average toddler's favorite animal. We go to the local zoo frequently, and they have lots of free-ranging peacocks. They are friendly and will walk right up to us, especially if my toddler happens to be eating goldfish crackers and is willing to share. I think this close interaction with peacocks from a young age made Maya favor them.

As Maya gets a little older, her imagination is really starting to come out. Her recent game of pretending involves grabbing Nathan or I and running to hide in our closet.

She will push me in the closet and shut the door behind her saying in a very concerned voice, "Mommy, there's a peacock out there!"

"Oh, do we need to hide from it?" I ask.

"Yes, it's going to bite me on the knee!" she answers, blocking the door so I can't get out. The only way to escape is for me to scare them away, but she seems to always have lots of peacock reinforcement just waiting to descend upon us once more. This is not my favorite game we play, but it is a testament to the strong imagination of children—truly believing in things that they cannot see.

Read

Now faith is confidence in what we hope for and assurance about what we do not see. This is what the ancients were commended for. By faith we understand that the universe was formed at God's command, so that what is seen was not made out of what was visible.

—Hebrews 11:1–3 NIV

Apply

As adults, we depend on our senses to tell us what is reliable. We want to see it, touch it, and fully experience it before we trust it. Unfortunately, being a Christian requires faith, the faith of a child who has complete confidence in the existence of something that is absolutely intangible. It isn't a blind faith, though, and these verses explain that so eloquently. God, in his infinite wisdom, created everything that we see, touch, and interact with everyday from absolutely nothing. All of that creation is a living testimony to the creator who brought it into existence.

The reason that we desire to rely on the tangible is because God created the tangible as proof that he is superior to it. If we can trust what we see, then how much more can we have confidence in the One who created it! Our assurance is a faith in the unseen, but is well-founded in the most reliable being we could ever know.

Pray

Father, I apologize for the times that I place my trust in created things before you, the creator. Help me to trust in you, believing the unseen is more secure than the tangible.

Reflect

How can I put my faith into action today?

Day Twenty Six

Sleepless with Distraction

When Maya was a baby, I counted down the minutes until nap time. She was a terrible napper, and I was lucky to get twenty minutes to myself. Everly doesn't nap on a typical baby schedule either, but that is because she has Maya to entertain her all the time. She rarely goes down for very long in the mornings because of her sister's constant entertainment. However, Maya eventually goes down for her nap after lunch. Everly crashes immediately and will sleep until Maya wakes up, usually around two hours later. As soon as her active distraction is gone and there is peace in the house, Everly goes out like a light. I love these tandem naps! When both girls sleep, they finally allow me to enjoy some peace and quiet.

Read

Then David ordered all the leaders of Israel to help his son Solomon. He said to them, "Is not the Lord your God with you? And has he not granted you rest on every side? For he has given the inhabitants of the land into my hands, and the land is subject to the Lord and to his people. Now devote your heart and soul to seeking the Lord your God. Begin to build the sanctuary of the Lord God, so that you may bring the ark of the covenant of the Lord and the sacred articles belonging to God into the temple that will be built for the Name of the Lord."
                                                        —*1 Chronicles 22:17–19 NIV*

Apply As Christians, our walk with Christ will go through many different seasons. In some seasons we may face a lot of opposition, while in other seasons, God will give us peace on every side. In the times of blessing, when we are experiencing smooth sailing, it can be tempting to let down our guard, relax our efforts, and slack on our spiritual disciplines. We essentially drift off to sleep, not feeling the needs that cause us to pray fervently or the threats to our faith that require us to scour God's Word for answers.

David and his son Solomon were experiencing a time of peace such as this in the kingdom of Israel, but instead of pulling back their efforts, they recognized that this time was crucial. Only in the time of peace could they construct a temple that would be a home of worship for God for generations. They took full advantage of the season of calm to build in anticipation of the coming trials in the future. In our current time, the temple of God is our very bodies, and we have the same calling to use our efforts in the peaceful times to build up our worship to be able to glorify God in the coming trials.

Pray Father, thank you for blessing me with seasons of peace in which you give me rest on every side. Give me the energy and ambition to continue to strengthen my spiritual disciplines even more so in the calm. Give me the recollection to use them when this season of calm has passed.

Reflect How can I use the time in this season for God's glory?

I Want My Wubby!

Maya calls her pacifier a wubby. We are slowly trying to decrease her dependence on her wubbies, but it is proving to be a tough habit to break. There are still two times when she really relies on them—when she is sleeping and when she gets hurt.

She will not go to bed or nap without the comfort of her pacifier, and if she loses it in the middle of the night, I will hear her call out, "I need my wubby!" I get up and feel around in her crib for it in the dark. Once I put it in her hand, Maya rolls over and goes right back to sleep.

Similarly, when I see Maya fall down and get hurt, I come running to scoop her up and check the damage. She always immediately wails, "I want my wubby!" In her crying voice, this sounds very much like, "I want my Mommy," but I have made that mistake too many times.

I hold her close and say, "I'm right here," only have her push me away and say, "No! Wubby!" I guess she doesn't realize that the wubby is just a piece of plastic—it can't help her or care for her. However, as her mother, I can and always will.

Read   *Be careful not to forget the covenant of the Lord your God that*
he made with you; do not make for yourselves an idol in the
form of anything the Lord your God has forbidden. For the Lord your God is a
consuming fire, a jealous God. [In the lands God will scatter you] you will worship
man-made gods of wood and stone, which cannot see or hear or eat or smell. But
if from there you seek the Lord your God, you will find him if you seek him with all
your heart and with all your soul. For the Lord your God is a merciful God; he will
not abandon or destroy you or forget the covenant with your ancestors, which he
confirmed to them by oath.

—Deuteronomy 4:23–24, 28–29, 31 NIV

Apply   While we may not have any carved idols in our
homes, there is a simple way to tell what we worship
—where do we turn first for comfort in times of distress? Is it a
screen? Food or drink? A behavior or habit? A relationship? The truth
is that we all have idols in our lives, things that we turn to in times of
need, seeking comfort and relief. Meanwhile, our Father is waiting,
arms open wide, with all of the resources and the desire to fulfill our
needs. The wonderful promise in these verses is that no matter how
many times we turn to other things first, and no matter which things
we turn to, as soon as we turn back to God, he will always be there
waiting to embrace us. He will never abandon us!

Pray   Father, thank you for your patience, waiting for me to
seek you wholeheartedly. Give me the strength to
turn to you first, rather than to something else, to give me comfort.

Reflect   What do I turn to first when trials come?

That's Bright

Maya sleeps with black out curtains in her room—my thinly veiled attempt to get her to sleep a little later in the mornings. At night, her room is like a black hole with no light anywhere. Sometimes in the morning when I go to get Maya out of her crib, I find her ready to play with an agenda in mind. She will immediately ask me to turn on the light for her.

I warn her, "Cover you eyes, it's going to be bright." She will close her eyes and put her little hands over them. I'll flip the switch, and she will slowly remove her hands, squinting in the light.

"That's bright, Mommy," she always says groggily. After her eyes have adjusted to the darkness all night, any light seems glaringly harsh in contrast.

Read *Do everything without grumbling or arguing, so that you may become blameless and pure, "children of God without fault in a warped and crooked generation." Then you will shine among them like stars in the sky as you hold firmly to the word of life. And then I will be able to boast on the day of Christ that I did not run or labor in vain. But even if I am being poured out like a drink offering on the sacrifice and service coming from your faith, I am glad and rejoice with all of you. So you too should be glad and rejoice with me.*

—Philippians 2:14–18 NIV

Apply Some things that Jesus teaches, when put into practice, are so glaringly different from the world that when they are demonstrated within our culture, it is starkly bright in contrast. The lesson laid out in these verses definitely falls into this category. The world is full of grumbling and complaining. It is so tempting to jump on the bandwagon rather than pursue a life that is blameless and pure. Rising above the natural reaction to demand our rights and seek justice, vengeance, or compensation, Jesus calls us to be willing to sacrifice and serve with joy.

Not only are we called to submit in this way while refraining from outward comment, but we are also called to live in such a way that it is accomplished with genuine rejoicing! The only way to truly achieve joy in unfairness is to hold firmly to God's Word, allowing it to reveal to us the true, eternal priorities of Christ. When we work with these goals in mind, it will cause a dark world to cover their eyes at the brightness of the glory of Christ displayed in our lives.

Pray Father, thank you for giving me the example of Christ, willing to give up everything in sacrifice to save me. I pray that when the urge to complain arises, I will remember his sacrifice and seek to live in a similar way with joy.

Reflect How can I serve in joy today?

_____

_____

_____

Evie Hungry Again

When Everly was a newborn, she ate frequently and for long periods of time, like most babies. I was prepared for this since Maya had been the same way. Maya, however, was not prepared for this. She was not a fan of the fact that I couldn't play with her constantly but had to take frequent breaks to feed the baby.

I can understand how frustrated she was with the constant interruptions to her usually unhindered time with Mommy. After a week or two, Maya started to understand the connection between Everly crying and me having to take a break from playing to feed her.

One day as Everly started to fuss, Maya threw her hands up in frustration, "Evie hungry AGAIN!" Trust me, in the middle of the night, I tend to have the same reaction.

Read

Jesus answered her, "If you knew the gift of God and who it is that asks you for a drink, you would have asked him and he would have given you living water."

"Sir," the woman said, "you have nothing to draw with and the well is deep. Where can you get this living water? Are you greater than our father Jacob, who gave us the well and drank from it himself, as did also his sons and his livestock?" Jesus answered, "Everyone who drinks this water will be thirsty again, but

whoever drinks the water I give them will never thirst. Indeed, the water I give
them will become in them a spring of water welling up to eternal life."

—*John 4:10–14 NIV*

Apply   In this life we have a lot of needs—physical needs for air, food, and water, emotional needs for love and a sense of belonging, and a spiritual need for an eternal purpose. Some of those needs must be filled again and again, but there is one need that Christ fills in our lives once, and it never runs dry. When we fill our spiritual need with devotion to God and surrender to Christ, we fill our lives with the living water that is the wellspring of life for our souls.

Interestingly enough, when our spiritual need is filled in this way, then our other needs are affected as well. We place ourselves in a position of trust when it comes to our physical needs, and we find our emotional needs met in him as well. Without Christ, we go through life asking everyone we come into contact with to fill us up. However, when we find our fulfillment in Christ and place our identity in him, we are filled to overflowing and can splash onto those around us!

Pray   Father, I choose to find my fulfillment in Christ. Fill me so that I can spread your amazing love with those around me. Thank you for loving me and promising to take care of my needs. Thank you for sending Jesus so that I can have a life flowing with living water.

Reflect   What need can I trust God to fulfill in my life today?

Day Thirty

I Want a Sip

Every morning Nathan makes coffee. He fixes his coffee mug up with the creamer first before pouring the coffee in. Inevitably one day, Maya asked him for a sip. The last thing that an active toddler like Maya needs is a caffeinated beverage. Instead of giving her a sip of coffee, he let her have a sip of his french vanilla creamer. Her eyes lit up at the taste!

"You like it?" he asked her.

"Mmm, hmm!" she said, "May I have some more?" It didn't take long before Nathan and Maya had a morning routine of making coffee together and him giving her a sip of creamer each morning.

Every morning at breakfast, Maya never fails to remind him, "Daddy, I want a sip!"

Read

When the dew was gone, thin flakes like frost on the ground appeared on the desert floor. When the Israelites saw it, they said to each other, "What is it?" For they did not know what it was. Moses said to them, "It is the bread the Lord has given you to eat. This is what the Lord has commanded: 'Everyone is to gather as much as they need. Take an omer for each person you have in your tent.'"

The Israelites did as they were told; some gathered much, some little. And when they measured it by the omer, the one who gathered much did not have too much, and the one who gathered little did not have too little. Everyone had

gathered just as much as they needed. The people of Israel called the bread
manna. It was white like coriander seed and tasted like wafers made with honey.

—Exodus 16:14–18, 31 NIV

Apply God, as our Father, sets a beautiful example of provision with manna in the Old Testament. Each and every day, all of God's children had enough, not too much and not too little, but the amount that they needed. God provided this sweet manna for them every day for the entire forty years that they wandered in the desert. If they tried to keep some for the next day, it would spoil. This day-by-day supply for their needs created a relationship of continual dependence on God.

We are called to the same kind of dependence today. We must come before the Lord morning by morning, allowing him to give us what we need for the struggles of the day. While our salvation is secure, we require continual sustenance in our day-to-day, and God has laid it out right before us in his Word. All we have to do is gather what we need.

Pray Father, thank you for being available to provide for my daily needs. Give me the discipline to turn to you for sustenance and provision each day.

Reflect How do I need God to provide for me today?

_____

_____

_____

_____

Look at Me

One of the most frequent phrases I use with Maya is "look at me." When I give her a set of instructions, I want to make sure she is listening. And then I know that she knows what I said, and I can hold her accountable for those directions. Sometimes, if Maya wants to tell me something but she isn't sure that I am listening, she will grab my face in her hands so that we are looking eye to eye. When someone looks me in the eye, even without saying anything, that person shares an unspoken understanding with me.

After having Maya, and even more so after Everly was born, I began to notice that I never really looked other adults in the eye. It didn't matter if it was a playdate with a friend and her kids, spending time with family members, or visits with friends at church, I would have whole conversations with one eye on Maya and one eye on Everly, and never look at the person that I was having a dialogue with. I would always leave these interactions feeling like the conversation had never actually happened because my attention had been so divided. Eye contact creates a meaningful connection that keeps interruptions and distractions at bay.

Read

I lift up my eyes to you, to you who sit enthroned in heaven. As the eyes of slaves look to the hand of their master, as the eyes of a female slave look to the hand of her mistress, so our eyes look to the Lord our God, till he shows us his mercy.

—*Psalm 123:12 NIV*

Apply I love the image in these verses of a slave looking to their master. As we live our lives, we need to turn our faces away from the many distractions that surround us and intentionally turn our eyes to Christ. We need to be constantly waiting, anticipating what he will ask of us next and eager to obey. The truth is that even as distracted moms, God has plans for us. He has a role for us to play in his story, in this season. But if we are looking the other way, we will miss his important instructions for us.

There are a lot of distractions for moms, a lot of things to do, and a lot of people demanding our attention. The struggle is real to spend time reading the Bible with a mind that isn't focusing on other things even as our eyes skim the words. The same can happen in our prayer lives—our minds focusing on the tasks of the day rather than looking into the face of our Lord. We cannot underestimate the power of taking the time to look into the eyes of Christ!

Pray Father, thank you for allowing me to have an intimate relationship with you in which you desire to see me face to face. Help me to prioritize and treasure a time to look you in the eyes every day.

Reflect How can I turn my face to the Lord today?

_____

_____

Day Thirty Two

The Cows are Sleeping

Near our house there is a large field with some cows in it. There are several different fields that they rotate the cows between, and only one of them is near the road where the animals can be seen. Maya loves to look for the cows every time we drive by and is always disappointed when they aren't out where she can see them. The first time Maya noticed that they were gone, she asked me where they were.

Instead of attempting to explain field rotation to my toddler, I simply said, "Maybe they are sleeping." Now every time she sees the field, Maya comments on whether or not the cows are sleeping.

After several weeks of this, Maya added one day, "Mommy, those cows like to sleep a lot!"

Read

I lift up my eyes to the mountains—where does my help come from? My help comes from the Lord, the Maker of heaven and earth. He will not let your foot slip—he who watches over you will not slumber; indeed, he who watches over Israel will neither slumber nor sleep. The Lord watches over you—the Lord is your shade at your right hand; the sun will not harm you by day, nor the moon by night. The Lord will keep you from all harm—he will watch over your life; the Lord will watch over your coming and going both now and forevermore.

—Psalm 121 NIV

Apply We all go through seasons when God seems distant, and we may be tempted to think that he is asleep, or far away, or even uninterested. This is simply not true. The truth is that God is vigilant, watching over us in every season, protecting us from harm, and equipping us for the struggles that we will face. This is good news because as much as our culture celebrates independence, we cannot watch over all of the details of our lives on our own, nor were we meant to.

We can rest in the promise that he will never stop watching over us and that no detail of our lives goes unnoticed. Not only does he see us, but he loves us because he made us, and therefore intimately cares about every aspect of our lives. In order to experience peace in the trials of this life, we must trust that God is in control of it all and that he is on our side. We must allow ourselves to be weak, so that he can be strong.

Pray Father, thank you for your promise to always watch over me and protect me. Help me to embrace a posture of dependence on you, trusting you to take care of me.

Reflect In what area of my life do I need to trust God to watch over for me?

Puddle Jumper

At the beginning of the summer, I was wondering how Maya would do in the pool. I got her a puddle jumper and was surprised how she took to the water like a fish. She wanted to be completely independent—swimming all around the pool by herself, jumping off the side into my arms, and even going off of the diving board! I was so proud of my fearless little girl!

Then one day, she was playing on the steps without her puddle jumper on, slipped, and went under the water. She bounced back up after just a second, coughing and crying. I gathered her onto my lap and explained that she needs her floaties to be able to go in the water by herself. For the rest of the summer, she approached the pool completely differently. Even with her puddle jumper on, Maya clung to my hand and stayed close to the steps. No matter how many times she listened to me explain that she would be fine as long as she wore the floaties, Maya had learned what the possibilities were when it came to the pool.

Read

Lord, if it's you," Peter replied, "tell me to come to you on the water."

"Come," he said. Then Peter got down out of the boat, walked on the water and came toward Jesus.

But when he saw the wind, he was afraid and, beginning to sink, cried out,
"Lord, save me!"

Immediately Jesus reached out his hand and caught him. "You of little faith,"
he said, "why did you doubt?"

And when they climbed into the boat, the wind died down. Then those
who were in the boat worshiped him, saying, "Truly you are the Son of God."

—Matthew 14:28–33 NIV

Apply We are so much like Peter! We want to be a part of what God is doing, asking to come out to him in the edgy, risky aspects of ministry, and he is happy to allow us to be a part of his work. However, many times once we begin to understand the full scale and scope of what we are a part of, we realize that we can't complete what we have started on our own. We begin to question if we have taken on too much and gotten in over our heads. Our doubts cause us to sink, and understandable so!

The truth is, we are too weak to finish the tasks ahead of us. We are involved in things far beyond our abilities. However, the only reason that we begin to sink is that we forget one vital factor—we aren't alone. We are out on the water with Christ. We are called to follow him, even if it is into water over our heads. In order to succeed, we must trust that with Christ at our side, we will be able to do the impossible!

Pray Father, thank you for allowing me to be a part of the work for your kingdom. Give me the courage to follow you wherever you lead and the humility to know that I reach the other side because of your hand.

Reflect In what task do I need to trust Christ as I continue working?

Sisterly Love

At five months and twenty eight months respectively, Everly and Maya are just starting to play together. Everly is starting to sit up, and Maya will throw a blanket over her head and then pull it off shouting "peek-a-boo!" Everly has this great baby belly laugh, sometimes laughing so hard that she topples over to the floor in her unsteadiness while sitting.

It is practically impossible not to start laughing when watching Everly's exuberant joy. Maya laughs along with her, jumping up and down, dancing, and making funny faces to get Everly to keep giggling. Seeing the two of them together in this way makes my heart so full! My most frequent prayer for them as sisters has always been that they love each other. When I see the two little girls that I love most in the world loving each other, nothing can top it.

Read

We love because he first loved us. Whoever claims to love God yet hates a brother or sister is a liar. For whoever does not love their brother and sister, whom they have seen, cannot love God, whom they have not seen. And he has given us this command: Anyone who loves God must also love their brother and sister.

—1 John 4:19–21 NIV

Apply God, as our Heavenly Father, gives his greatest command for us in relation to each other in this one rule: love one another. Every person that we come into contact with is God's creation, and when we show love to his children, we are showing love to him. While loving others does not always come easily, we have been well-equipped to love others by the extravagant love that God has lavished on us.

When we think about the lengths that God went to, giving his own Son to die in order to give us an opportunity to receive his love, it is overwhelming! How could we not share this amazing love with others? This radical love is not only life changing, but also lifestyle changing, putting us in a position to lavish love on others.

Pray Father, thank you for the amazing love that you have shown me by withholding nothing from me in an effort to redeem my life. Allow me to offer the same grace and love to your children that I come into contact with today.

Reflect Who is God calling me to love, and how can I do that today?

_____

_____

_____

_____

_____

I Know, I Be Very Careful

Maya is a daredevil. She loves climbing, jumping, and especially climbing tall things and jumping off. As a mom, I sometimes feel like a broken record, saying the same few instructions over and over again.

One day when Maya was jumping on the sofa, I started with my usual set of instructions, "Maya...."

Before I could get past the first word, she stopped jumping and held up her hand to quiet me, "I know, Mommy. I be very careful. I not want to fall down and go boom on the head." I was speechless. I must have told her that a hundred times, and for the first time, I knew she had heard me and understood the risks involved. Unfortunately, it didn't seem to stop her in the least from thinking that she could continue without any consequences.

Read *I have hidden your word in my heart that I might not sin against you. Praise be to you, Lord; teach me your decrees. With my lips I recount all the laws that come from your mouth. I rejoice in following your statutes as one rejoices in great riches. I meditate on your precepts and consider your ways. I delight in your decrees; I will not neglect your word.*

—Psalm 119:11–16 NIV

Apply In the same way that we love hearing our children repeat the instructions we have taught them (and even more so when they act on them), God loves when we delight in his Word. We should know scripture so well, from reading it over and over, that it comes out of our mouths without any hesitation. If we are putting his Word into our lives daily, then we can't help but have his voice in our hearts at all times.

When we hear a lie, God's truth will spring to our minds in defense. When we are tempted to sin, God's boundaries will help us turn away. When we lose our identity, his promises will stir in our hearts. When we face trials, his eternal perspective will give us the courage to continue forward. When we know the Word well, and we live our lives accordingly, we can use it for the kingdom.

Pray Father, give me a love for your Word. Allow me to hide it in my heart so that I can use it to protect and guide me as I go along the path you set before me. Allow your truth to come to my mind and mouth when I need it.

Reflect Choose a verse or set of verses to begin to commit to memory today.

_____

_____

_____

_____

_____

Not Just Take That Away

Maya's deepest surge of feeling injustice comes out when I take something away from her. It doesn't matter if I warn her ahead of time that I'm going to have to take it. She doesn't care if I am taking it as a consequence of an action. Sometimes, the thing I am taking isn't even hers, and I have to give it back to someone else that she took it from. The specific scenario doesn't matter. If I take something away, she is indignant.

"Not just take that away!" she yells. Sometimes she even holds something out to give to me, and when I reach to take it, she yanks it back in disbelief that I would even consider doing such a thing! The sense of something belonging to her apparently started early and strong.

Read *Consider it pure joy, my brothers and sisters, whenever you face trials of many kinds, because you know that the testing of your faith produces perseverance. Let perseverance finish its work so that you may be mature and complete, not lacking anything. If any of you lacks wisdom, you should ask God, who gives generously to all without finding fault, and it will be given to you.*

—James 1:2-5 NIV

Apply   Most of the trials that we face in life involve a loss. It could be the loss of someone we love. It could be the loss of something, such as a physical possession. It could be the loss of an ability or our health. Maybe it is the loss of a position within our family, job, or church. We can even lose a perception such as our identity or reputation. How many times do we get angry with God when he takes something away from us?

Rather than thanking our Father for being the one who gave it to us in the first place, we tend to only focus on the fact that we no longer have it. While it is difficult to have this perspective in the midst of releasing something, we must remember that God uses these seasons of receiving and releasing to grow us into the likeness of Christ. The only way to become mature is to grow through these seasons of loss and allow ourselves to let go of the good in order to receive the best, trusting in God's enduring love for us.

Pray   Father, I am sorry if I have allowed myself to blame you for a loss rather than thanking you for the many blessings in my life. Help me to see how I can grow in each loss as it comes and to trust that you have my best interests in mind.

Reflect   What am I holding on to that I need to release today?

_____

_____

_____

_____

Making Me Nervous

One night when she was eating dinner, Maya looked at me and said, "These peas are making me nervous." I had never heard her use the word "nervous" before.

"What?" I asked, thinking that I must have misunderstood her.

"I'm working on it, but these peas are making me nervous," she repeated with a worried look. In spite of myself, I started laughing. I know that I'm not supposed to take my child's fears and feelings lightly, but the idea was just so ridiculous. I know that she learned the phrase from me constantly telling her that she makes me nervous when she is climbing on the furniture. Thankfully, the peas seemed to make her less nervous as the meal went on, and she discovered that she could pile them into the indention on the top of her sippy cup.

Read

And do not set your heart on what you will eat or drink; do not worry about it. For the pagan world runs after all such things, and your Father knows that you need them. But seek his kingdom, and these things will be given to you as well.

—Luke 12:29–31 NIV

Apply I have a feeling that when we put some of our fears into words, God has a laugh as well. While our fears matter to God and may seem overwhelming to us, they are insignificant in the scheme of his power in our lives. The thing is, God knows what we need, and he has promised to care for us. When we begin to worry, it is because our attention is on the wrong things.

God calls us to spend our time and energy focusing on the eternal, spiritual matters that are intangible. When we see our daily needs in the light of eternity, we begin to see them as God sees them—not worth worrying about. Focusing attention on earthly needs is an occupation best left to those who only have a temporary kingdom to build. Thankfully, our kingdom is in heaven!

Pray Father, help me to identify my fears and release them to you. Give me peace in situations where I tend to worry, and help me to focus on eternal things instead. Allow me to confidently place my trust in you, knowing that you will provide.

Reflect What worry do I need to entrust to God today?

_____

_____

_____

_____

_____

I Just Have To

Kids are definitely born with a personality. There are some things that they just *have* to do. Maya loves climbing on things and jumping off. I'm not sure how this became her favorite pastime. I certainly don't go around climbing all over everything and jumping off as an example. She simply had it in her head to do it. I can tell by the look in her eyes when she is considering jumping off of something or climbing something, which is good because sometimes I need to curb her enthusiasm. The other day she climbed into her playhouse and was standing at the top of the ladder, looking down at the ground with that familiar look in her eye.

"Maya, don't jump from there! It's too high. Just climb down the ladder," I instructed.

She looked at me and gave her best effort at rational toddler reasoning, "But Mommy, I just have to." Great. I know that in her little soul, she just *has* to climb things and jump. She just has to.

Read   *Dear friends, let us love one another, for love comes from God. Everyone who loves has been born of God and knows God. Whoever does not love does not know God, because God is love. This is how God showed his love among us: He sent his one and only Son into the world that we might live through him. This is love: not that we loved God, but that he loved us and sent his Son as an atoning sacrifice for our sins. Dear friends, since God so loved us, we also ought to love one another. No one has ever seen God; but if we love one another, God lives in us and his love is made complete in us.*

—1 John 4:7–12 NIV

Apply In the same way that Maya has an innate need and desire for feeling the pull of gravity as she plummets to the ground, God even more so has a character that cannot be shaken or altered. It is easy for us to sometimes question why God loves us when we continue to make mistake after mistake. We wonder why he would give up something as precious as his own Son to offer us forgiveness. We question if he really continues to love us even when we openly turn our backs on him. The answer is simple—he just has to because God is love. God doesn't simply love others or have a loving character. He is the absolute definition of love. God and love cannot be separated. Therefore, nothing we do can ever separate us from his love. Why does he love us? He just has to!

Pray Father, thank you for being love! Thank you for loving me, and allow me to experience that love in all of its purity, with no strings attached, so that I can in turn love others in the same way. Help me to love myself in the way that you love me.

Reflect How have I questioned God's love for me?

_____

_____

_____

I Said Please

We have been teaching Maya to ask for the things that she wants and say 'please' rather than whining or crying. The other day she wanted to go swimming in her kiddie pool in the backyard, but it was thundering and lightning outside. She asked me, and I told her no.

"Mommy, may I *pleeeease* go swimming?" she asked again, stressing the 'please.'

"No, Maya. You already asked me, and I gave you my answer. Asking again isn't going to change my answer, so do not ask me again."

She looked confused, and replied, "But Mommy, I said please." I decided to try using logic.

"Yes, you did say please, and I like your good manners, but you can't play in the water while it's lightning outside. It can be dangerous."

She looked at me blankly and then fell to the ground flailing and crying, "But I want to!" I should have known that logic wouldn't work with a two year old.

Read

This is the confidence we have in approaching God: that if we ask anything according to his will, he hears us. And if we know that he hears us—whatever we ask—we know that we have what we asked of him.

—*1 John 5:14-15 NIV*

Apply   When we pray, we tend to think that the answer to our prayer somehow depends on the way that we ask. If we say the right words, say it very sincerely, say it in a certain holy place or have the purest of motivations, then God will grant us our desire. The truth is that God is not a genie granting three wishes to those who say 'please.' He has no limitations in lavishing even seemingly impossible blessings on those he chooses. He also has no required quota that he must meet with a 'yes.' It is pretty simple—God hears us when we are praying in accordance with his will.

Unfortunately, he does not reveal his will as readily as we would like. While this can seem frustrating in many ways, it is so comforting in others. We can rest in the confidence that when God answers our prayers, we know that we are within his will. In the same way that Gideon believed the signs that God confirmed for him, we can trust that God will lead us in the way that we should go within his will.

Pray   Father, thank you for listening when I pray to you. I apologize for the times that I have treated prayer like a wish list, and I rest in the confidence that you will respond to my requests when they are in accordance with your will.

Reflect   What is one answer to prayer that I am still waiting to hear from God?

Day Forty

Tummy Time

As a baby, Maya hated tummy time. I can count on one hand the number of times she did it, because she would wail from the moment I put her belly on the floor until I would finally pick her up again. She disliked it so much that at only two months old, she learned to roll from her belly to her back, so that she could face up again. My curious little girl couldn't stand having her face to the floor.

What Maya didn't know is that being on her back would never lead to anything more than just looking around. In order for her to learn how to crawl, pull up, and eventually walk, she would have to start on her belly. While being on her belly made her feel stuck, Maya could only experience all of the freedom that life has to offer by starting on her belly. Unfortunately, simply being on her belly would not get her moving. It would require lots of practicing, slowly growing stronger, learning how to flex the right muscles to achieve the desired movement, and eventually, lots of falling down.

Read

This is what the Lord says: "When seventy years are completed for Babylon, I will come to you and fulfill my good promise to bring you back to this place. For I know the plans I have for you," declares the Lord, "plans to prosper you and not to harm you, plans to give you hope and a future. Then you will call on me and come and pray to me, and I will listen to you. You will seek me and find me when you seek me with all your heart. I will be found by you," declares the Lord, "and will bring you back from captivity. I will gather you from all the nations and places where I have banished you," declares the Lord, "and will bring you back to the place from which I carried you into exile."

—Jeremiah 29:10–13 NIV

Apply There are two popular verses in this text, surrounded by some others that are usually left out. Why? The Israelites were being banished into exile in Babylon when God gives this incredible promise for their future. While they clung to this promise, it was still seventy years in the future for them. I'm sure they felt like they had been sentenced to pointless waiting.

There are times that we may ask ourselves why God has us in a certain position in life. We may feel trapped, immobile, stuck, or even exiled without any way to move forward. Only God knows the purpose behind each season of our lives. He knows which skills he has for us to learn in that place, which practices we need to ingrain, and which attitudes we need to cultivate in order to prepare us for the new levels of independence we will graduate to in the future. Only in exile did the Israelites reach out to God and seek him fully. God has us where we are for a reason, and it is for our good.

Pray Father, thank you that you have good plans for my life! I pray that you will help me to trust you in the seasons that seem so far from where I want to be. Help me to be open to learning and growing so that I can reach where you call me.

Reflect How do I need to be growing in this season?

New Playground

    Maya went through a phase where she was constantly asking for new things. If she had a sippy cup, she wanted a new sippy cup. If she was wearing a dress, she wanted to change clothes and put on a new dress. If we were going to play at the playground, she wanted to go to a new playground.

    During this phase I scouted out every random school, church, and community playground that was open and put them on a big rotation so that we could go to a 'new' playground as often as possible. In a toddler's ever-growing world with a sponge-like ability to take in new experiences, sometimes something new is necessary. Even with the playground rotation, Maya caught on quickly to the fact that the playgrounds we were visiting were not actually new. Thankfully, she decided that mostly new was new enough for her.

Read

Create in me a pure heart, O God, and renew a steadfast spirit within me. Do not cast me from your presence or take your Holy Spirit from me. Restore to me the joy of your salvation and grant me a willing spirit, to sustain me.

—Psalm 51:10–12 NIV

Therefore, if anyone is in Christ, the new creation has come: The old has gone, the new is here!

—2 Corinthians 5:17 NIV

Apply   We all like renovating old things to make them look new, but sometimes it is necessary to start over completely. When it comes to our hearts, unlike Maya's playground choices, mostly new won't do; we need a full transplant. The good news is that through the cross, Jesus offers exactly that.

When we commit our lives to Jesus, completely surrendering the old, and committing to follow in his plan for us, we become new! While we will still struggle with sin, we are a new creation in Christ, blameless in the eyes of God, and ready to share in eternity with him. If we simply try our best to clean our hearts on our own, we will struggle endlessly to no avail. The only way to truly achieve redemption is by grace through faith in Jesus Christ alone.

Pray   Father, thank you for the offer of a new heart through Jesus. Help me to stop striving to achieve forgiveness by being good, but rather give me the humility to surrender my desires for your will each day.

Reflect   How do I try to make myself new on my own?

_____

_____

_____

Day Forty Two

Keep Your Shoes On

One day I may break down and super glue Maya's shoes on her feet. There is something about sitting in a car seat with nothing to do that makes her immediately take off her shoes.

Sometimes she will ask, "Mommy, I can take my shoes off?"

If we are headed home, I will tell her 'yes,' but if we are going anywhere else, I will tell her, "No, keep your shoes on; you are going to need them when we get there." Even with the explanation, I almost always hear the sound of velcro and shoes hitting the floor of the car within seconds of my instructions.

Many times, I just put her shoes in the car, not on her feet, knowing that I'll just be putting them on again when we get to our destination. This is not the ideal situation, though, because that means I have one more step when getting the kids out of the car. In addition to all the car seat buckles, strollers, and diaper bags, I also have to track down shoes. If we needed to get out in a hurry, it wouldn't happen. Without her shoes on, Maya is simply not prepared.

Read

Be dressed ready for service and keep your lamps burning, like servants waiting for their master to return from a wedding banquet, so that when he comes and knocks they can immediately open the door for him. It will be good for those servants whose master finds them watching when he comes. But understand this: If the owner of the house had known at what hour the thief was coming, he would not have let his house be broken into. You also must be ready, because the Son of Man will come at an hour when you do not expect him."

—Luke 12:35–37a, 39–40 NIV

Apply We never know what will be required of us in our daily Christian lives. Maybe a friend will ask us about our faith. Maybe an interaction with a stranger will test our self-control. Maybe the day's demands will wear down our Christ-like attitude. If we enter each day assuming that we can handle its demands on our own, we might as well leave home without our shoes. We must anticipate these unexpected events with careful spiritual preparation. We must approach each situation with prayer and dependence on God. Then we can be sure that whatever comes our way, we will be well-equipped to handle it in a way that honors Christ.

Pray Father, thank you for not only including me in the plans to advance your kingdom, but also for equipping me to handle what you call me to do. Help me to depend on you and prepare for every situation through continual prayer and surrender.

Reflect What daily routine will help me to be prepared at all times?

Contagious

When Everly was born, and we headed home from the hospital, we couldn't wait to be reunited with Maya at home. Instead, we got a call from my in-laws that Maya was running a 103 degree fever. I had lots of worries all at once. What did Maya have? How was she doing being sick away from me? Maya had visited Everly in the hospital! Would Everly get sick at only two days old? RSV or flu could be fatal to a newborn!

One thing was clear, we could not put the two girls together until Maya was fever-free for at least two days. I stayed with Everly at my parents house, and Nathan stayed with Maya at our house until she was no longer contagious. It ended up being a stomach virus, and we were able to unite as a family of four a week later.

Read *Do not be yoked together with unbelievers. For what do righteousness and wickedness have in common? Or what fellowship can light have with darkness? What harmony is there between Christ and Belial? Or what does a believer have in common with an unbeliever? What agreement is there between the temple of God and idols? For we are the temple of the living God. As God has said: "I will live with them and walk among them, and I will be their God, and they will be my people." Therefore, "Come out from them and be separate," says the Lord.* —2 Corinthians 6:14–17a NIV

Apply As Christians, we are called to reach into the dark places and engage in a world of sin while still living in accordance with a different standard than that of the world. However, there are some limits that we need to put in place in certain circumstances. In the same way that Everly was too vulnerable as a baby to risk being exposed to a virus, if we are new Christians or if we struggle with certain past addictions or habits, we need to guard ourselves against exposure to them.

God tells us to draw a line when it comes to entering into a partnership of any kind with unbelievers. Being yoked with an unbeliever can take many forms—a business partnership, a spouse, a friend that you rely on for advice, or a counselor or mentor. Allowing people who live in darkness to have a place of authority, leadership, or counsel over your personal thoughts and actions is an outbreak waiting to happen. Sometimes, separation is necessary for the health of a Christ-follower.

Pray Father, thank you for freeing me from the sin of this world. Give me your wisdom and discernment as I choose which voices to allow to influence my thoughts and decisions. Give me the strength to reach out to those different from me without fear, but also limit exposure to unbelievers who pull me from you.

Reflect From which toxic influence do I need to separate myself today?

Frenemies

I never really understood the concept of frenemies until Maya had one. A good friend of mine and I meet each week, and her three-year-old son and Maya play while we visit. While each of our children get along fine with other kids, when the two of them are together, they immediately start pushing each others' buttons. Maya will find a treasure on the ground, such as a feather.

Zander will hold out his hand, "It's my turn, you have to give it to me!"

"No," she'll yell at him. After a second she'll hold it out right in front of him to tempt him with it. When he goes to grab it, she'll snatch it back, "Not take it away from me!"

"Don't yell in my face!" he'll reply, holding his hand out to create some personal space.

"Not push me!" she'll shout back pushing his hand to the side. They purposely set each other off, and it is pretty exhausting. And yet, every time we finish playing, Maya says, "I like playing with Zander. Zander is my friend!" You could have fooled me!

Read

Do not repay anyone evil for evil. Be careful to do what is right in the eyes of everyone. If it is possible, as far as it depends on you, live at peace with everyone. Do not take revenge, my dear friends, but leave room for God's wrath, for it is written: "It is mine to avenge; I will repay," says the Lord.

—Romans 12:17–19 NIV

Apply   Much like toddlers, we tend to be quick to stand up for our rights, reinforcing our boundaries, and defending our own causes. While our culture celebrates this defense of liberty, we quickly forget that Jesus lived with very different priorities. Rather than protecting his own rights, he protected the rights of others. He did not take revenge on those who murdered him, but rather asked his Father to forgive them.

If we are to live as Christ lived, we must seek to make peace with those around us. The most interesting irony of living defensively is that we tend to most often react negatively to those we love, our family and friends, rather than our enemies. In the end, our fierce self-protection only serves to alienate us from those who are our truest advocates. While the work is not easy, we must strive to repay evil with good.

Pray   Father, allow me to release any defensiveness that I have when it comes to protecting my own rights. Help me believe that you will be the one to avenge me. Allow me to forgive those who hurt me and live at peace with those around me.

Reflect   What infringement of my rights do I need to let go of?

_____

_____

Day Forty Five

Little Gifts

Maya loves to leave little gifts for Nathan and I all over. Sometimes I will find her baby doll tucked under the covers of my side of the bed. Looking for a pen in my purse one Sunday morning, I found a spoon that Maya had put in there for me. How thoughtful! I never know when I will need a spoon!

Once when Nathan went on a business trip, he found that she had packed two pacifiers in the top of his bag. I frequently find things in my shoes when I go to put them on—a piece of play food or a crayon. No matter how impractical these gifts are, they make me smile every time I find one. These small tokens of love are reminders that she is thinking of me, and I love finding them.

Read

For since the creation of the world God's invisible qualities—his eternal power and divine nature—have been clearly seen, being understood from what has been made, so that people are without excuse.

—Romans 1:20 NIV

I have set my rainbow in the clouds, and it will be the sign of the covenant between me and the earth. Whenever I bring clouds over the earth and the rainbow appears in the clouds, I will remember my covenant between me and you and all living creatures of every kind. Never again will the waters become a flood to destroy all life.

—Genesis 9:13–15 NIV

Apply In the same way that Maya leaves tokens of her love for me to find, God has created an entire world filled with his beauty and his character revealed from the tiniest details to the vastest unknowns. So much of who he is and what he has promised is all around us. With this display in creation, God is waiting for us to continually discover new facets of who he is and how he loves us.

Sometimes God reveals a reminder of a covenant that he has made with us, such as a rainbow. Sometimes it is simply a creation that teaches us something about the creator. Finally, other times, it is something very personal and intimate, a small surprise meant just for us from God. From the enormity of the universe to the intricacy of DNA, the evidence that God is thinking of us is never far and is sure to make us smile.

Pray Father, thank you for revealing yourself to us through your creation. Thank you for the many signs that you give just for me to show me how much you love and care for me.

Reflect In what way have I seen a sign of God's love lately?

_____

_____

_____

_____

_____

Day
Forty
Six

Putting on Shoes

Oh, it's the daily battle of putting on the shoes. Instead of going for her super-easy velcro shoes, Maya has discovered her black buckle shoes in the back of the closet where I had hidden them.

"No Mommy, not help me! I can do it by myself!" she waves her hands at me to stay away. I sigh, back off, and change Everly's diaper in the other room. I hear the silence that comes with her focusing on a task. I hear her huffing in frustration. Now there's growling and grunting.

Inevitably follows the stomping of the feet, and finally Maya calls out, "Mommy, I can't do it! I need help!" I go in the room. She has the wrong foot halfway shoved into one shoe, her hair disheveled, and her cheeks red.

I take one tentative step toward her, the way one might approach disarming a bomb, "I can help you."

"No!" she screams, "Not touch it! I can do it!" I step back. "I need help," she whines in despair, flinging one shoe to the ground in frustration. This really is a dramatic tragedy in the making!

"Are you ready for help now?" I ask before approaching.

"Yes," she finally concedes, defeated. We work together to put on the shoes, and all is well...until tomorrow, when we will do all this again.

Read   *If my people, who are called by my name, will humble*
themselves and pray and seek my face and turn from their
wicked ways, then I will hear from heaven, and I will forgive their sin and will heal
their land. Now my eyes will be open and my ears attentive to the prayers offered
in this place.

—*2 Chronicles 7:14–15 NIV*

Apply   We love our independence, and there are few things
more satisfying than being able to do something on
our own. The problem comes when we refuse to accept that we are
simply not capable of handling even the smallest of trials that life
throws at us without God's help. In the same way that I can't
understand why Maya won't simply let me help her, God is
expressing the same question in these verses. He is telling us that he
has all of the answers, all of the capability, and the desire to help us
no matter the situation. Yet, we look the other way and get
frustrated when we can't accomplish the desired results on our own.

    He is waiting for us to surrender control so that he can step in
and heal our hearts and our land. The key is to humble ourselves and
take responsibility for the part that we have played, confessing our
sins. When we do that, God is quick to act on our behalf.

Pray   Father, give me the humility to turn to you in my time
of need, refusing to give in to the lie that I am capable
of working out of sin on my own.

Reflect   How can I humble myself in God's presence today?

Day Forty Seven

What's That Smell?

As I took the bag of dirty diapers out of the diaper pail, I noticed something out of the ordinary. Through the clear bag, I saw something black and pink in between the layers of white diapers. What was that? I got a pair of scissors and cut a small hole in the bag near the object and took it out. It was Maya's water shoe. So that's where that went! I threw away the bag of diapers and then took a sniff of the shoe. Oh my goodness! It reeked of number two!

I quickly put it into a load of laundry and then stuffed a dryer sheet into it before I put it into the dryer. I took it out and gave it a sniff, but it still smelled horrendous. Until I could decide my next course of action to attempt to save the shoe, I put it outside on the back porch to air out, and I promptly forgot all about it. The next day when we stepped out the back door to play outside, I was overcome by the smell of poo. I was about to start checking all the kids' diapers when I realized that it was the water shoe! I tried several other methods of getting the smell out, but eventually, I threw it away.

Read

But thanks be to God, who always leads us as captives in Christ's triumphal procession and uses us to spread the aroma of the knowledge of him everywhere. For we are to God the pleasing aroma of Christ among those who are being saved and those who are perishing. To the one we are an aroma that brings death; to the other, an aroma that brings life.

—2 Corinthians 2:14–16 NIV

Apply It can be confusing to think about how being an example of Christ can be an aroma of life to some people and an aroma of death to others. But this water shoe helps make it all clear. While the smell of poop on Maya's water shoe was an unwelcome one to me, the same smell to a gardener putting manure on her plants would be a very welcome one. The smell of manure is evidence of the life-giving nutrients being put into the soil for the growth of new plant life. There is no difference in the smell, only the perspective of the person who is smelling it.

When we demonstrate an example of Christ to non-Christians with our lives and they react confrontationally, it should come as no surprise. Even if we are acting in love and not judgement, our very love is perceived as condemnation because their lifestyle and actions are completely opposite. Meanwhile, the same demonstration of Christ's love to those who accept it is the very essence of life. This knowledge of truth allows them to experience all of the freedom that comes from a new life in Christ. We should never allow others' reactions to hold us back from spreading the aroma of Christ everywhere we go. It quickly reveals the hearts of those around us!

Pray Father, thank you for giving me a part to play by spreading your aroma to those around me. Give me the strength to continue this work even when I encounter opposition.

Reflect How can I be the aroma of Christ to others?

Trick Riding

Maya has a rocking horse that she likes to practice trick riding on. She will stand on its back with her arms stretched out to either side, then say, "Watch, Mommy!" as she slowly lifts one foot in the air until it is all the way out the side up to shoulder height. She also practices her dismounts, of course. Jumping off is her favorite, and sometimes she adds a half twist or a flair with her hands of some kind.

While I'm watching, I try very hard not to see all of the things that could happen. Unlike me, Maya has limited experience with gravity and doesn't see anything wrong with trying all kinds of new tricks. In her mind, the limitations are simply not there. In time, after she falls more frequently with her more risky moves, she will begin to learn where the line is between what she can and can't do. For now, I am constantly amazed at her lack of inhibition and her daring approach to life!

Read

"Have faith in God," Jesus answered. "Truly I tell you, if anyone says to this mountain, 'Go, throw yourself into the sea,' and does not doubt in their heart but believes that what they say will happen, it will be done for them. Therefore I tell you, whatever you ask for in prayer, believe that you have received it, and it will be yours.
                                                                —Mark 11:22–24 NIV

Apply As we get older, we learn our own limitations as well as the limitations of the world that we live in. The problem is that our minds apply these same limitations to God. While we know intellectually that the one who created everything isn't limited by the parameters of his creation, we tend to forget that fact when it comes to matters of faith. Jesus teaches in these verses that all that is holding us back from overthrowing the very laws of nature is our belief that it can't be done.

As a result, many times in prayer, we don't pray for what we truly desire, afraid that it is unlikely to happen. Rather than praying for healing, we pray for peace. Rather than daring to ask for a miracle, we ask for God's will to be done. These prayers are not wrong, but they lack faith. How would our prayer lives look different if we lived in the belief that the impossible is within our grasp? In order to truly believe that God can do anything and act on that belief in our everyday walk with Christ, we must return to the faith of a child who doesn't comprehend gravity.

Pray Father, I'm sorry for the ways that I have placed limitations on you by not having faith. Give me the faith to pray courageously, believing that all things are possible.

Reflect In what way have I placed a limitation on God's abilities in my mind?

Getting Dressed

When it comes to getting dressed, toddlers have their own ideas, and Maya is as unique as they come. While she still struggles with getting dressed by herself, she is very adept at taking off her clothes and diaper without any help. If I go to change Everly's diaper or feed her and leave Maya alone in her room, I never know what I will return to see.

Sometimes, she is wearing her rain boots on the wrong feet, upside down sunglasses, a winter hat, and nothing else. Another day, she may be wearing her swimming floaties, an apron from her play kitchen, a big bow in her hair, and a pair of my shoes.

"I ready to go," she'll announce. Little does she understand that she is far from ready to enter the day without at least a diaper on! While she is all about the frivolous accessories that make her look pretty, she consistently overlooks the necessary basics.

Read

Therefore put on the full armor of God, so that when the day of evil comes, you may be able to stand your ground, and after you have done everything, to stand. Stand firm then, with the belt of truth buckled around your waist, with the breastplate of righteousness in place, and with your feet fitted with the readiness that comes from the gospel of peace. In addition to all this, take up the shield of faith, with which you can extinguish all the flaming arrows of the evil one. Take the helmet of salvation and the sword of the Spirit, which is the word of God.

—*Ephesians 6:13–17 NIV*

Apply

As absurd as we adults may find Maya's outfits, we tend to have the same approach to preparing for the day. We wouldn't dream of leaving without brushing our teeth, putting on deodorant, and wearing a somewhat coordinated outfit, complete with shoes. However, how many times do we walk out the door without putting on the character traits and spiritual protection that we will need to stand firm in our convictions throughout the day? We have an arsenal of weapons and armor to prepare us for the battle that rages around us. The catch is that it only helps us if we have the discipline to put each piece into place.

Pray

Father, thank you for providing me with everything that I need to overcome the trials and temptations of each day. Help me to develop the discipline needed to take the time to prepare spiritually.

Reflect

How can I create a routine to truly prepare for each day?

_____

_____

_____

_____

_____

_____

Day Fifty

I'm That Mom

Before I had kids, I worked in children's ministry, and I had this hilarious idea that since I could handle a large group of kids well that I would one day be an excellent mom. I learned something really fast—being a full-time mom to even one child is way more difficult than teaching a whole group of someone else's kids. Anyway, I never thought that I would be *that* mom. You know, the one who the church nursery volunteer sees walking up on a Sunday morning and thinks, *Oh gosh. She's here. We're going to need an extra volunteer for her daughter.*

To say that Maya did not appreciate being dropped in her class at church is an understatement. I'm pretty sure there was a solid year of Sundays in which Maya cried the entire time until we were called to get her. I would sit in church with my cell phone on my knee, waiting to get the inevitable text. But no matter how many times I had to pick her up from class and dry her tears, I was always willing to do it again, because she is my daughter, and I love her.

Read

"Therefore say: 'This is what the Sovereign Lord says: I will gather you from the nations and bring you back from the countries where you have been scattered, and I will give you back the land of

Israel again.' "They will return to it and remove all its vile images and detestable idols. I will give them an undivided heart and put a new spirit in them; I will remove from them their heart of stone and give them a heart of flesh. Then they will follow my decrees and be careful to keep my laws. They will be my people, and I will be their God.

—*Ezekiel 11:17–20 NIV*

Apply You know what? Our God is *that* God. The one who comes after us no matter how many times we stray, how far we go, or how much we pitch a fit. He is always willing to bring us back from no matter where we have wandered. It isn't his fault that we never seem to learn our lesson and consistently turn away from his truth and then cry out until we are rescued.

Thankfully, the truth of the matter is that we are God's children, and he will never stop pursuing us because he loves us. When Satan sees us do something wrong, he would like nothing more than to convince us that there is no way that God could forgive us. The enemy wants us to believe that God is tired of dealing with our continual failures. Nothing could be further from the truth. He is *that* God, who pursues us endlessly.

Pray Father, thank you for never giving up on me, but always being willing to bring me back to yourself when I call out to you. Thank you for promising to give me a heart of flesh in place of my heart of stone.

Reflect How has God gathered me back to him in the past?

_____

_____

Day Fifty One

Love in Time Out

Anyone who says that kids are not manipulative has not met Maya. In our Cajun French culture, we call it "canaille" (kah-NIGH), which basically means sneaky or doing something with ulterior motives. Maya loves to employ her skills of manipulation most when she is facing a consequence. When she has to go to time out, she may suddenly need to go potty, be absolutely dying of thirst, or unexpectedly experience pain of some kind that needs immediate attention. The other day she had to go to time out for not listening (we are forever working on first-time obedience.) She was strangely cooperative for once.

As she sat in the appointed chair for the allotted two minutes, Maya started sweetly singing to herself, "Jesus loves me this I know, for the Bible tells me so." I couldn't help but laugh. Whether the song was a coincidence or she was trying to stir up some grace in me, I'm not sure. Either way, I couldn't help but think about how she was spot on.

Read

You see, at just the right time, when we were still powerless, Christ died for the ungodly. Very rarely will anyone die for a righteous person, though for a good person someone might possibly dare to die. But God demonstrates his own love for us in this: While we were still sinners,

Christ died for us. Since we have now been justified by his blood, how much more shall we be saved from God's wrath through him! For if, while we were God's enemies, we were reconciled to him through the death of his Son, how much more, having been reconciled, shall we be saved through his life! Not only is this so, but we also boast in God through our Lord Jesus Christ, through whom we have now received reconciliation.

—*Romans 5:6–11 NIV*

Apply We can have the same assurance of Jesus' love that Maya does. At the very height of our disobedience, God still loved us so much that he allowed Jesus to take on the punishment for that sin. He doesn't love us any more or less based on how we respond to this sacrifice. He went through with it without any requirement for us to accept this redemption. Of course, he waits in anticipation that we might repent and be saved, but there were no strings attached when Jesus died for us. Even when we are experiencing the consequences of our sins, we can still have confidence that God loves us. Once we do accept Jesus' sacrifice and surrender our lives to him, we can only boast in what Jesus has done for us. It certainly isn't earned by anything that we have done. When God looks at us in all of our mess, he sees Jesus' perfection instead!

Pray Father, thank you for loving me when I was still far from you. Thank you for giving me the choice to follow you and experience freedom from sin. Help me to remember that no matter what mess I am in, I can be confident of your love.

Reflect How do I believe that I am beyond God's ability to love?

Babymoon

Nathan and I took a babymoon to Iceland for four days when I was seven months pregnant with Everly, and Maya was nineteen months old. It was the first time we had ever left her overnight. We had a wonderful trip, and I controlled my emotions about leaving Maya pretty well for a mom. On our way home, I was missing my little girl and definitely ready to see her again.

In the New York airport, an out-of-season freeze in Atlanta caused a cancellation of practically all flights. We spent the next three days trying to get home. We rebooked flights so many times that at the end of the first day we had twenty-two different boarding passes. We ended up taking an Uber from New York to New Jersey, flying to Chicago, then to Dallas, then to Houston, and the plan was to rent a car and drive home to Louisiana from there.

At the car rental desk, we were informed that they did not accept debit cards. I was done. We had been in airports longer than we had been in Iceland. I hadn't seen my daughter in a week, we hadn't slept in two days, and I was a pregnant, hormonal wreck. I cried quite dramatically at the counter, and they finally found a loophole in a rewards program in which we could rent the car. We drove home, and I had never been so happy to see Maya in my life!

Read

Then Jesus told them this parable: "Suppose one of you has a hundred sheep and loses one of them. Doesn't he leave the ninety-nine in the open country and go after the lost sheep until he finds it? And when he finds it, he joyfully puts it on his shoulders and goes home. Then he calls his friends and neighbors together and says, 'Rejoice with me; I have found my lost sheep.' I tell you that in the same way there will be more rejoicing in heaven over one sinner who repents than over ninety-nine righteous persons who do not need to repent.

—Luke 15:3–7 NIV

Apply

I would have walked all the way home if it had been the only way to get to my daughter. In the same way, God will do whatever it takes to make a way to bring us back to him when we wander off. In the parable above, the shepherd leaves all of the other sheep and searches until the lost one is found. Through the sacrifice of Jesus on the cross, God found the loophole in justice to offer us grace. When Jesus rose to life on the third day, he overcame the spiritual laws of the universe to create a possibility for us to return to him. I can't think of a much more dramatic way to demonstrate just how much God loves us. And yet, we still listen to Satan's lie that God could not possibly love us. Have no doubts about the persistence of his extravagant love!

Pray

Father, I am overwhelmed by the depth of your love for me. Allow me to live confidently in that love, be able to accept it in my life, and extend it to others in response

Reflect

In what way does Satan convince me that I am unloved?

Day Fifty Three

Another Night

A typical night at my house (last night, to be exact):

7:36pm- Maya goes to bed after one book (aka four books.)

8:08pm- Everly goes to bed after diaper change, pajamas, final eat, burping, and rocking.

10:05pm- I go to bed after spending some time cleaning up and hanging out with Nathan.

1:45am- Everly wakes up wanting to eat. Trying to train her to sleep longer stretches between feedings, I rock her back to sleep without feeding her. (It works!)

2:38am- Everly wakes up, figures out she's been tricked, and is determined that it won't happen again. I feed her. I can't get her to burp after the second side.

4:47am- Everly wakes up, ready to burp now.

6:07am- Maya wakes up and can't find her pacifier. I find it and convince her it is still night.

6:36am- Everly wakes up hungry for breakfast. I have to force myself out of bed. I walk into Everly's room, and her whole face lights up with the brightest smile. It's going to be a good day!

Read

Do you not know? Have you not heard? The Lord is the everlasting God, the Creator of the ends of the earth. He will not grow tired or weary, and his understanding no one can fathom. He gives strength to the weary and increases the power of the weak. Even youths grow tired and weary, and young men stumble and fall; but those who hope in the Lord will renew their strength. They will soar on wings like eagles; they will run and not grow weary, they will walk and not be faint.

—Isaiah 40:28–31 NIV

Apply   Life is tiresome, and we are weary, but we can be encouraged that the God we serve never tires. Not only that, but he is eager to pass his strength and energy on to us when we hope in him. God doesn't simply offer the endurance to make it through another day, he gives us the strength to run, to fly, to thrive! Our minds can't seem to comprehend how our increasing weakness results in his increasing strength, but these verses tell us that we shouldn't bother trying to fathom his understanding.

When we surrender to God in our weakness, he is strong and swift to carry us through not only to completion, but to victory. This is the day that the Lord has made, and his purposes will be accomplished in spite of our human limitations. Today is going to be a good day!

Pray   Father, thank you for promising to give me the energy to complete the tasks that you have laid before me in each season. Help me to depend on you for the strength that I need in times of weakness.

Reflect   In what situation do I need God's endurance and energy today?

Milk- It Does a Body Good

The way that God created a mother's body to naturally protect and provide for her baby astounds me. Everly is the most kissable baby in the world (at least, to me.) I can't seem to get enough of kissing her round cheeks, her squishy toes, and her tiny fingers.

Did you know that there is a scientific reason behind this? When I kiss my baby's face and hands, I am exposed to any germs that may be on her. My body then creates antibodies to fight those specific germs, and those antibodies are delivered to Everly through my breast milk. Isn't that so amazing?

In this way, whatever she is exposed to, I am exposed to. Any harmful germs she experiences, I experience. Because of this shared contact with the same harmful pathogens, I am prepared to help her overcome their influence by giving her what she needs to successfully fight them.

Read

In your relationships with one another, have the same mindset as Christ Jesus: Who, being in very nature God, did not consider equality with God something to be used to his own advantage; rather, he made himself nothing by taking the very nature of a servant, being made in human likeness. And being found in appearance as a man, he humbled himself by becoming obedient to death—even death on a cross!

—Philippians 2:5–8 NIV

Apply Sometimes, we are tempted to think that the wisdom of the Bible doesn't apply to us in our current situation because God doesn't truly understand what we are going through. We couldn't be further from the truth. Jesus, God himself, came down from heaven, leaving his place of deity, and took on human flesh. He lived life on this earth. He experienced pain, loss, betrayal, love, friendship, and temptation. He had his reputation smeared, his teachings questioned, and his trust broken. He was respected, despised, loved, and hated. He experienced hunger, thirst, joy, and exhaustion.

There is nothing we face that he has not faced, and therefore, nothing that he cannot help us overcome. The particulars may be different, but there is no one who can better empathize with us in our struggles or give us better strength to fight through. He has been exposed to all of the same pathogens of this world, and he has the antibodies. Isn't that so amazing?

Pray Father, thank you for sending Jesus to become a human like me, so that I can trust that he understands what I am going through on a personal level. Help me to turn to Christ when I am struggling in a situation, and give me the courage to act on the guidance and wisdom you give to make it through.

Reflect What is one situation I can entrust to Jesus today, knowing that he can empathize?

I Not Going to Touch It

We were building a pergola in the backyard one weekend. This makes for an ideal, safe, exploratory environment for a toddler—ladders, power tools, lumber, metal hardware, etc. We spent most of the day telling Maya not to touch anything. There was a large plastic bucket full of screws that she was particularly interested in.

"Remember, Maya, do not touch that," I said authoritatively.

"I not going to touch it," she answered very convincingly with a wave of her little hands, "I just going to look at it."

"Okay," I conceded, "you can look at it." She inched slowly towards the bucket and peered inside. She crouched down next to it and shuffled even closer until her knees almost touched the side of the container. She leaned forward, putting her face right down into the bucket, so close that I could see condensation from her breath on the side of the plastic in the humid summer heat. While she was obeying what I had said, Maya was going as close to the line as she possibly could without crossing it. She was playing with fire, setting herself up to fall in the face of overwhelming temptation.

Read

When tempted, no one should say, "God is tempting me." For God cannot be tempted by evil, nor does he tempt anyone; but each person is tempted when they are dragged away by their own evil desire and enticed. Then, after desire has conceived, it gives birth to sin; and sin, when it is full-grown, gives birth to death.

—*James 1:13–15 NIV*

Apply   We know what particular things and attitudes are temptations for us. It could be food, worry, binge watching Netflix, gossip, fear, doubt, shopping online, jealousy, comparison, vanity, greed, and so on. While we would love to place some of the blame on God for allowing us to come into contact with these temptations at all, it is actually just us who allow ourselves to be enticed. We get in close proximity to the temptation and then try to bolster our self-control while inching nearer to it. We think that just being close, but not taking part, won't harm us.

We call a friend who is a known gossip and don't bother to stop them when the conversation gets juicy. We click on the ad for that cute outfit, determined to look but not buy. We let Netflix continue to the next episode without turning it off. At the risk of oversimplifying, it's time for us to just stop it! The first step to overcoming temptation is to stay far, far away. Thankfully, we know that God is here to help us and will never set us up for failure.

Pray   Father, give me the discipline to stay far away from the temptations that I'm most sensitive to. Help me to take responsibility when I put myself into tempting situations and take the initiative to remove myself from the situation.

Reflect   What temptations do I need to actively avoid?

Can I Get a Witness?

The other day, we were listening to a song on the radio that had the line, "Can I get a witness?"

We were singing along and being goofy, so my husband turned to Maya and said, "Maya, can I get a witness?"

Without skipping a beat, she answered, "Yeah! I get you a witness, Daddy!" She ran to her play kitchen, pretended to make something, and came back with an imaginary thing in her hand.

"Here's your witness, Daddy!" she beamed, holding out her empty hands to him.

Of course, we laughed as he pretended to gobble it up. "Mm, that's a good witness! Thank you, Maya!"

Read

"A man named Ananias came to see me [Saul/ Paul]. He was a devout observer of the law and highly respected by all the Jews living there. He stood beside me and said, 'Brother Saul, receive your sight!' And at that very moment I was able to see him. "Then he said: 'The God of our ancestors has chosen you to know his will and to see the Righteous One and to hear words from his mouth. You will be his witness to all people of what you have seen and heard. And now what are you waiting for? Get up, be baptized and wash your sins away, calling on his name.'

—Acts 22:12–16 NIV

Apply Unfortunately, like Maya, we sometimes don't really know what being a witness looks like. In these verses, Saul (later to be Paul) is receiving back his sight after being blinded on the road to Damascus. He is finally turning to be a witness for Christ, rather than a persecutor of those who follow Christ. I love how simply Ananias describes what it means to be a witness—we know God's will, we hear his words, and then we tell everyone about that.

Being a witness indicates a sense of complicity—we are in the know about what God is up to, and we are taking part in it. Unfortunately, being a witness isn't something that we can turn on or off. As Christians, everything that we do is a testimony to the life that we have received in Christ, especially when we think no one is watching. We must take care to represent the name and work of God with all of the respect that it deserves.

Pray Father, thank you for giving me a role in your work on earth as a witness. Help me to take advantage of every opportunity that you place before me to share with others what I have learned about you. Allow others to see a picture of your character in my everyday life.

Reflect How can I be a witness for Christ today?

_____

_____

_____

Day Fifty Seven

Let's Exercise!

Every now and then Maya uses a word, and I have no idea where she would have heard anyone say it. I am always amazed at her ever-growing vocabulary.

One day while she was playing in the backyard, and I was working in the garden, Maya ran over to me in a very enthusiastic mood, "Mommy, come exercise with me! It's going to be so much fun! Woohoo!" Exercise? Where in the world did she learn that word? I realize that my astonishment says a lot about my relationship to exercise, and I'm okay with that. I was curious to see what she had determined exercise to be and why she was so excited about it. I took off my gardening gloves and followed her to the playhouse.

"We are going to climb up the slide, and climb down," she explained, still very animated, "That is our exercise!" We climbed up the slide, and slid back down the slide. Anytime I play on a child-sized play thing, it definitely counts as exercise. But Maya was right —we had a lot of fun!

Read

Therefore, my dear friends, as you have always obeyed—not only in my presence, but now much more in my absence—

continue to work out your salvation with fear and trembling, for it is God who works in you to will and to act in order to fulfill his good purpose.

—*Philippians 2:12–13 NIV*

Apply As much as I am not an exercise person, there is some work that we need to put into our salvation. Wait! I thought we were saved by grace, through faith, and not by our works. Yes! These verses aren't saying that we need to work out how to be saved (thank goodness), but rather to work out that salvation in our lives.

This can be tedious work, searching for areas of our lives in which we are not wholly committed to Christ and laying them down over and over. It is a discipline, a daily exercise, that we need to take seriously for our spiritual health. But we don't have to be overwhelmed, because we have God as our personal trainer. He has the end result in mind, and that result is good! He will not stop working in our lives until his work has reached completion!

Pray Father, help me to develop the habit of working out my salvation, constantly seeking ways to become more like Christ and devoting my life to you. Thank you for having a plan for me to continue in this work and for having a good purpose for my life.

Reflect What is one area in which I need to work out my salvation?

We Having a Tea Party!

Girls must be born with a tea party gene. I don't drink tea. My husband rarely drinks tea. And yet, we have a lot of tea parties at our house. These spontaneous parties can happen anytime, anywhere, and with a surprising variety of objects used as tea cups.

Maya can find a flower outside and say, "This my decoration! We having a tea party!" And so it begins. When it comes to preparation, Maya doesn't cut any corners. There are guests to invite, food and tea to prepare, and decorations to be set up. She makes sure to bring me a cup of tea, that has obviously been made with care, on a little platter.

With a big smile, she'll say, "Here your tea, Mommy. Just drink it." She did not learn this from me. Hospitality is at the bottom of my spiritual gifts list. But I do make sure to gush over how delicious her tea is.

Read

Offer hospitality to one another without grumbling. Each of you should use whatever gift you have received to serve others, as faithful stewards of God's grace in its various forms. If anyone speaks, they should do so as one who speaks the very words of God. If anyone serves, they should do

so with the strength God provides, so that in all things God may be praised
through Jesus Christ. To him be the glory and the power for ever and ever. Amen.

—1 Peter 4:9–11 NIV

Apply While my idea of hospitality is remembering to offer water to someone who visits, there is hope. These verses explain that we can show hospitality by offering whatever our gifts are. We all have been given gifts and talents from God with which we can serve the church and those around us. The key isn't what we do, but the attitude with which we do it. In order to use our gifts with the correct motivation, we must depend on God's leading.

While Maya's tea is actually pretend, her earnestness and care in serving it is real. When we allow ourselves to work in God's strength, we can provide for real needs all around us, whether physical, emotional, or spiritual. When we serve in the way he has gifted us and in his power, we inevitably bring him glory and exhibit his hospitality to the world.

Pray Father, thank you for giving me gifts with which I can share your love with the world. Help me to develop and use those gifts for your glory, depending on your power. Help me to keep the focus of these works on you and not fall into selfish motivation.

Reflect What are my gifts and how can I use them?

_____

_____

_____

_____

Day Fifty Nine

When it Rains

One thing I love about south Louisiana in the summer is big thunderstorms. Come to think of it, that may be the only thing I love about south Louisiana in the summer. I love the feeling outside right before a storm. The sky turns darker and darker, and the wind starts to whip in intermittent bursts and gusts. Thunder vibrates the ground as it rumbles in the distance, and the birds begin flying back to their nests with calls to one another. It seems as if all of nature is waiting in anticipation, almost holding its breath until the skies open in a sudden downpour. These kinds of storms don't start with a sprinkle, it is more like turning on a faucet. One day, we were playing outside as one of these storms began to stir.

I told Maya, "It is about to rain, and when it does it is going to start really fast. We can play until it rains, but when I say so, you need to run as fast as you can to the porch, okay?"

"Yes, Mommy," she answered.

After a few minutes, the skies open up, "Okay, Maya, run!" I yelled as I snatched Everly out of her swing and ran to the porch. I reached the porch and put Everly down, looking back to see Maya standing in the rain crying, right where I had left her. I ran back out in the rain, picked her up and hurried back under the porch with her, both of us soaking wet.

Read   *We know that the whole creation has been groaning as in the pains of childbirth right up to the present time. Not only so, but we ourselves, who have the firstfruits of the Spirit, groan inwardly as we wait eagerly for our adoption to sonship, the redemption of our bodies. For in this hope we were saved. But hope that is seen is no hope at all. Who hopes for what they already have? But if we hope for what we do not yet have, we wait for it patiently.*
—Romans 8:22–25 NIV

Apply   In the same way that all of creation seemed to be waiting for the coming storm, in this life we are waiting for the final redemption on the last day. One day, Jesus is going to return triumphantly, and we will be reunited with him for eternity in paradise. Not only will we be redeemed, but all of creation as well. Everything that was affected by Adam and Eve's fall will be made new—a new heaven and a new earth.

Every now and then we experience moments in which we know that there is something more, and we yearn for it deep within our souls. It is coming. All of the signs are pointing to it. In the same way that I had warned Maya, the Bible tells us to be ready for the day when it arrives. We don't want to be left crying in the rain.

Pray   Father, thank you for the promise of something more! I look forward to the day of redemption with anticipation and pray that I will be ready when the time comes.

Reflect   How can I live in anticipation of redemption today?

_____

_____

Day Sixty

Feeling the Wind

I remember when Maya first felt wind. As a baby, she cried about eighty percent of the time. She had reflux and was just unhappy, but she really liked being outside. We spent a lot of time walking in the yard, looking at flowers, and watching the chickens peck around. One day, when she was about a month old, Maya was in my lap swinging on the porch swing hung from the big oak tree in the backyard, when a gust of wind blew.

She sucked in her breath suddenly, her short baby arms flailing at her sides. It had startled her, and she wasn't sure what to think. I suppose the wind on her face gave her the unsettling feeling of falling. Every time the wind would blow, Maya would gasp and clutch her little fists. After several gusts of wind, she began to react less each time, and soon she was enjoying the cool breeze that was a welcome respite from the stifling summer heat.

Read

When the day of Pentecost came, they were all together in one place. Suddenly a sound like the blowing of a violent wind came from heaven and filled the whole house where they were sitting. They saw what seemed to be tongues of fire that separated and came to rest on each of them. All

of them were filled with the Holy Spirit and began to speak in other tongues as the
Spirit enabled them. —Acts 2:1–4 NIV

Apply Maya had to learn what wind felt like without being afraid. In the same way, I'm sure the disciples weren't without their share of fear at the strange thing that was happening to them. However, in the power of the Holy Spirit, they were finally able to speak about Jesus without fear. The disciples went from hiding in a locked room to preaching on street corners.

The Holy Spirit is mysterious, but we don't have to be afraid. Learning to listen to the promptings of the Holy Spirit is a bit like learning to feel the wind. At first it is unexpected and harsh, then slowly we learn that it is a welcome and reliable replacement for trying to figure things out on our own. Learning to listen to the Spirit takes time, it takes consistency in saying 'yes' rather than ignoring it, and it takes silence. We must make sure that we leave margin in our lives for the Holy Spirit to fill. When we do, we develop the fruit of the Spirit: love, joy, peace, patience, goodness, gentleness, kindness, faithfulness, and self-control.

Pray Father, thank you that you did not leave me alone in this world, but have left the Holy Spirit to guide me. Help me to cultivate the habit of listening to and following the promptings of the Holy Spirit.

Reflect How can I create margin in my life and practice listening to the Holy Spirit?

Day Sixty One

Tandem Naps

Having two kids less than two years apart, I have one goal for each day. One purpose which, if accomplished, makes life so wonderful—tandem naps. Tandem napping is when both girls are asleep at the same time for any length of time. I'm not picky, even just ten minutes is appreciated.

The reality is that most days, Everly is on a two-nap-a-day schedule, and Maya is on a one-nap-a-day schedule, which puts them rarely napping at the same time. But every now and then, when the tandem nap happens, it is like the clouds part, the sun breaks through, and God smiles down on me! If only they could be united and like-minded when it comes to napping every day, what a wonderful world it would be!

Read *Therefore if you have any encouragement from being united with Christ, if any comfort from his love, if any common sharing in the Spirit, if any tenderness and compassion, then make my joy complete by being like-minded, having the same love, being one in spirit and of one mind. Do nothing out of selfish ambition or vain conceit. Rather, in humility value others above yourselves, not looking to your own interests but each of you to the interests of the others.*

—Philippians 2:1–4 NIV

Apply God has a similar request for us as his children—be like-minded, be unified in purpose, and love each other by putting one another first. Unfortunately, Christians are not known in the world for these characteristics. In fact, we are most commonly known by our segregation, differences of opinions, and disagreements. In these verses, Paul urges us to not focus on what can separate us into groups, but rather celebrate and rally behind what unites us.

The things we all have in common are our relationship in Christ, the presence of the Holy Spirit in our lives, and a first-hand understanding of God's love. Basically, Paul challenges us that if our new life in Christ is authentic, then we will be united in a way that crosses all cultures, countries, ages, socio-economic groups, political views, and barriers of any kind. We are one in Christ, so let's be like-minded! This is of the highest importance.

Pray Father, thank you for giving all who believe in Christ a common ground in which we can celebrate and unite. Help me to focus on the things that I have in common with other Christians when I am tempted to draw lines of division or take sides.

Reflect How have I contributed to division among believers? How can I focus on like-mindedness instead?

_____

_____

_____

_____

Day Sixty Two

Facing Out

Maya was born ten days after her due date. As a result, I'm pretty sure she was born with the strength of a ten day old, because she came out trying to hold up her head. From day one, Maya was a very observant baby. She wanted to see everything all the time.

Even as a newborn, she would not allow me to hold her chest to chest. She would crane her neck to look around and see what was happening. To keep from constantly trying to get her to stop wiggling around, I started carrying her facing out all the time, her back to my chest and my arm cradled under her thighs like a little seat. Snuggling was never a thing with Maya. If she wasn't facing out, she was pitching a fit.

Read

"I am sending you out like sheep among wolves. Therefore be as shrewd as snakes and as innocent as doves. Be on your guard; you will be handed over to the local councils and be flogged in the synagogues. On my account you will be brought before governors and kings as witnesses to them and to the Gentiles. But when they arrest you, do not worry about what to say or how to say it. At that time you will be given what to say, for it will not be you speaking, but the Spirit of your Father speaking through you.

—Matthew 10:16–20 NIV

Apply As Christians, we can sometimes spend a lot of time facing in to our own circles of friends and those who share our worldview. However, these verses warn us that we need to be "facing out" at the world, realizing that they do not share our values or convictions. We must be on our guard, ready to speak in the face of targeted abuse.

We shouldn't be surprised when we face opposition since the very King of kings, whose name we profess, was murdered for these same teachings. However, God gives us an incredible promise, not that we will be spared from persecution, but that when we are persecuted, we will bring glory to God by speaking the truth in his spirit. Our ultimate goal as Christians is not our own comfort, but his glory.

Pray Father, speak your truth through me today as I face out into a world that is lost. When persecution comes, help me to not focus on how I have been hurt, but rather how I can bring you glory in that situation. Keep me from focusing in on myself and my Christian community, but rather reach out into the darkness with your discernment.

Reflect How can I allow the Spirit of the Father to speak through me today?

_____

_____

_____

Day Sixty Three

Face First

It was one of those days in which Maya was feeling extra adventurous. We were planning on having dinner at my sister's house. I got Maya out of the car in the driveway. I had turned to get Everly out of her carseat when I heard splashing. I discovered Maya running full speed through a ditch between the yards with at least four inches of water in it.

"Weeee!" she cried as she ran the whole length of it with arms outstretched, kicking water up all over her third outfit of the day. (This explains why such a small person creates so much laundry!)

I sighed and grabbed the diaper bag for yet another change of clothes. She continued squealing and splashing in delight until she tripped and completely face-planted into the puddle. I mean, she didn't stop the fall in any way. It was absolutely face first followed by her whole body flat out in the water. She came up with a huge gasp for air and started crying, but no damage was done. Thankfully, wet clothes can be washed and dried.

Read

But now, this is what the Lord says—he who created you, Jacob, he who formed you, Israel: "Do not fear, for I have redeemed you; I have summoned you by name; you are mine. When you pass through the waters, I will be with you; and when you pass through the rivers, they will not sweep over you. When you walk through the fire, you will not be burned; the flames will not set you ablaze. For I am the Lord your God, the Holy One of Israel, your Savior.

—*Isaiah 43:1–3a NIV*

Apply As we go through life, we may have the opportunity to do some crazy, fun, and amazing things for God's kingdom. While serving him may sound like hard work sometimes (and it is), it can also be filled with the carefree and thrilling joy of a child running through a puddle. God created us to find joy in our walk with him and in our service for him.

There is a catch—you can't go through the puddles without getting wet. When we go through this life, there will be waters rising. There will be fire. There will be hardships, trials, and struggles. But God's amazing promise to us in these verses is that when we come against those things, no matter how completely we fall on our faces, it won't be detrimental. We will not be overcome. We will not be harmed beyond repair because God is with us. He picks us up again. We don't have to fear because he has called us to this work, and he has redeemed us for this work. He will not send us out alone—he is our Savior!

Pray Father, thank you for your incredible promise in these verses to call me to a higher purpose, protect me as I follow you in that purpose, and never leave my side when things get tough. Thank you for this reminder that I have nothing to fear!

Reflect How does this promise change my perspective on something that I usually fear?

Bedtime Finish Line

As a mom of littles, I essentially work for about fourteen hours a day and am on call for the other ten. It nevers stops. But bedtime, oh glorious bedtime, comes every day. God, in his infinite goodness, created day and night. We read the bedtime story, brush teeth, breastfeed, put on pajamas, change diapers, make an attempt on the big girl potty, say our prayers, sing the song, tuck them in, rock them, turn off the light, close the door, tiptoe away from the room with fingers crossed, and hold our breath.

And then, listen, do you hear it? Silence. Stillness. Breathe, we did it! They are asleep. Even though all they have to do is say "Mommy!" to snap me right back to the reality that they are still there, for a moment it feels like freedom. At the end of the day, I have nothing left to give. I have poured out all of my energy, my encouragement, my listening and responding, my correcting, my instructing, my facilitating of fun activities, and my overall being a sane person. I am D.O.N.E.

Read

But you, keep your head in all situations, endure hardship, do the work of an evangelist, discharge all the duties of your ministry. For I am already being poured out like a drink offering, and the time for my departure is near. I have fought the good fight, I have finished the race, I have kept the faith. Now there is in store for me the crown of righteousness, which the Lord, the righteous Judge, will award to me on that day—and not only to me, but also to all who have longed for his appearing.

—2 Timothy 4:5–7 NIV

Apply   In the same way that we have a pretty overwhelming task load as mothers, Paul has similar feelings about his duties as a Christ-follower. Paul, at the end of his life, looks back over his ministry and is happy to say that he has nothing left to give. He has poured out all of his energy, talents, and resources for the advancement of the kingdom, and he is ready for the finish line. Once we cross to the other side, it will be true freedom—a paradise in heaven where we commune with our Savior and worship our King.

The reward is worth the wait and worth the work, and when the time comes, I hope we too can say that we have nothing left to give. What does that look like in this season of life? I think Paul explains it perfectly in the first line—"keep your head in all situations, endure hardship, do the work of an evangelist, discharge all the duties of your ministry." The details will look different for each of us, but Paul is challenging us to finish well.

Pray   Father, give me the energy and endurance to pour out everything that I have for your kingdom. Thank you for the promise of an end with a reward worth working toward. Help me to finish well what I have started for you.

Reflect   In what specific way can I keep the faith today?

Broken Crayons Still Work

Maya likes coloring time, but not so much the actual coloring. She likes to look through her coloring books at all of the pictures. She likes to take her crayons in and out of the crayon container, over and over again. She likes lining all the crayons up on the carpet to make a train. She also likes jumping off of her chair and landing on top of a pile of crayons. As a result, she has quite a few broken crayons.

One day she held up the two crayons halves with a sad face and said, "It's broken!"

"It's okay," I told her, "They still work even if they're broken. See?" I took a crayon and colored on the paper.

"Oh," she brightened, "Now I have two crayons!" Seeing more crayons rather than broken ones is a great perspective!

Read *Blessed are the poor in spirit, for theirs is the kingdom of heaven. Blessed are those who mourn, for they will be comforted. Blessed are the meek, for they will inherit the earth. Blessed are those who hunger and thirst for righteousness, for they will be filled. Blessed are the merciful, for they will be shown mercy. Blessed are the pure in heart, for they will see God. Blessed are the peacemakers, for they will be called children of God. Blessed are those who are persecuted because of righteousness, for theirs is the kingdom of heaven.*

—Matthew 5:3–10 NIV

Apply   The Bible promises that in this life we will have trouble. It also promises that the hardships we experience will be used for good. Rather than looking at ourselves and seeing what is broken, we can read these verses and be reminded that God not only restores what is broken, but also has a special gift of blessing for those who experience it. Much like with crayons, brokenness does not keep us from being able to work. It allows us to work in new and different ways than we could before.

We experience brokenness in so many ways—broken relationships, degenerating health, loss of identity, rejection, betrayal, failure, lack of purpose, or financial insufficiency. Instead of focusing on how we are broken, we can find healing when we allow God to meet us in our weakness and heal our broken hearts so we can rise again with his abounding blessings. Here is the thing—we must let go of the brokenness. Sometimes we like being the victim. We enjoy carrying around our hurts rather than accepting that God has more for us once we are ready to move on. It is time to release the pain and walk in blessing!

Pray   Father, thank you for promising restoration and blessing in the areas where I experience brokenness. Help me to allow you to heal the broken places, letting go of the grip that I allow them to have on my life, and embrace the way in which you will use it for good.

Reflect   What area of brokenness do I need to release to God so I can grab hold of his blessings?

Day Sixty Six

She Knows Me

At less than a month old, Everly could differentiate between me as her mother and anyone else. In the following months, she has gotten to know me more and more to the point that she becomes distressed when someone else holds her. Sometimes people get offended that she is so fussy with anyone who was not her mother, but it only makes sense.

She and I are intimately connected. We have spent so much time together that she knows how I hold her, what I smell like, and what my voice sounds like. When I pick her up in her pitch dark room in the middle of the night, she immediately knows that it is me and quiets, resting in the comfort and security of her mother's arms.

Read

"Very truly I tell you Pharisees, anyone who does not enter the sheep pen by the gate, but climbs in by some other way, is a thief and a robber. The one who enters by the gate is the shepherd of the sheep. The gatekeeper opens the gate for him, and the sheep listen to his voice. He calls his own sheep by name and leads them out. When he has brought out all his own, he goes on ahead of them, and his sheep follow him because they know his voice. But they will never follow a stranger; in fact, they will run away from him because they do not recognize a stranger's voice."

—John 10:1–5 NIV

Apply Many times, we find ourselves asking, "How do I know the prompting of this thought is from God?" The question we are really asking is, "Do I know the shepherd's voice?" Jesus indicates in these verses that he makes himself intimately known to his followers. When we take the time to get to know him personally, we will know his voice in the same way a baby knows her mother's touch. His character will be so much a part of who we are that there will be no doubt.

Our concern for the truth in this matter is not misplaced because there are robbers and thieves trying to break into our hearts by roundabout methods. We must be careful to know our shepherd's voice well, so that we can distinguish it even in the darkest moments of life. Only then will we be able to follow him to safety and security, trusting in his care for us.

Pray Father, help me to know Jesus so intimately that I never mistake another's voice for his. Give me faith in his care to follow where he leads me, and give me the discernment to turn away from any influence that is not from him.

Reflect How can I become more familiar with Jesus' voice?

_____

_____

_____

_____

_____

Day
Sixty
Seven

Ultrasounds

One of the most incredible parts of pregnancy is having an ultrasound. It is amazing to me that we can look inside of the womb and see the tiny life growing there. I could watch those little hands grasping around, legs stretching, and body twisting all day long. In one of the ultrasounds, the lab tech looks at each organ to make sure that it is functioning properly. The heart pumping blood, the mouth swallowing fluid, and the kidneys working are all clearly visible.

The 3D ultrasounds are even more incredible. With Maya, we had a 3D picture taken during the second trimester ultrasound and when she was born, she looked just like the picture! I couldn't believe it! Seeing the baby so alive and precious inside of me is a special experience, and it brings to mind a certain set of verses every time.

Read   *For you created my inmost being; you knit me together in my mother's womb. I praise you because I am fearfully and wonderfully made; your works are wonderful, I know that full well. My frame was not hidden from you when I was made in the secret place, when I was woven together in the depths of the earth. Your eyes saw my unformed body; all the days ordained for me were written in your book before one of them came to be.*

—Psalm 139:13–16 NIV

Apply We seem to constantly struggle against the effect of the physical world on our bodies. We may desire to be prettier, thinner, stronger, healthier. We may struggle with life-long diseases, recurring sickness, or simply the weariness of the everyday grind. While our bodies are just a temporary shell, these verses reveal such a tender side of God as our creator and Father.

Our bodies were created with great care by the Artist of artists. Our stories were planned with the anticipation of a happy ending. We were born with the fingerprints of God all over our identity, and he delights in us as his wonderful creation. These verses promise us such love and purpose. How could we not rest in his wisdom and discernment about how he has designed each of us?

Pray Father, thank you for the care that you put into creating me! I choose to trust your wisdom in how you made me, knowing that you will use my unique self to further your kingdom here on earth until my body is renewed in eternity.

Reflect What do I need to accept about how God has created me?

_____

_____

_____

_____

_____

_____

Day Sixty Eight

Inside Voice

Right before she turned five months old, Everly began a new and terrible phase in which she hated riding in the car. From the time we would clip her in the car seat to the time she got out, she would give the loudest, most consistent, wailing moan sound.

"Aaaaaaah, aaaaaaah, aaaaaaah!"

Maya would sit in her car seat with her hands over her ears saying, "Shh, Evie! That's too loud!"

Meanwhile, I would try my hardest to pay attention to the road and not lose my mind. As with all things with kids, it was just for a season, and she stopped one day just as abruptly as she had started. The worst part about this particular phase was that I couldn't really do anything about it while driving. Even if I had been able to, a five month old is far too young to understand any kind of instruction on using an inside voice or to listen to my pleas to just stop already. I was powerless to take any action that would be effective.

Read

When we put bits into the mouths of the horses to make them obey us, we can guide the whole animal. Consider ships as well. Although they are so large and are driven by strong winds, they are steered by a very small rudder wherever the pilot is inclined. In the same way, the tongue is a small part of the body, but it boasts of great things. Consider how small a spark sets a great forest ablaze. The tongue also is a fire, a world of wickedness among the parts of the body. It pollutes the whole person, sets the course of his life on fire, and is itself set on fire by hell. All kinds of animals, birds, reptiles, and creatures of the sea are being tamed and have been tamed by man, but no man can tame the tongue. It is a restless evil, full of deadly poison.

—James 3:3–8 NIV

Apply Some things are difficult to control, but the Bible is pretty clear that the words that come out of our mouths (or that our fingers type) are at the top of this list. The tongue is so dangerous because it is underestimated. Something so small couldn't possibly create so much damage, right?

The popular teaching that "words will never hurt me" is a classic example of how our culture undermines the power the tongue holds. In order to begin to control our tongues, we must first understand the power it possesses to give life or death. If we know and respect the power of our words, we will be much more likely to weigh them carefully before letting any escape.

Pray Father, help me to begin to practice a more thoughtful approach to what I say before I open my mouth. Give me wisdom and guidance when using my words so that they will bring life rather than destruction to those around me.

Reflect What is one practical way that I can get better control over my tongue today?

_____

_____

_____

Day Sixty Nine

All of You From All of Me

I am grateful that I was able to exclusively breastfeed both of my girls. With Everly, I had an interesting revelation when she was around five months old. Right before we started introducing baby food, I was breastfeeding her one day, looking down at her sweet face, and her long body, marvelling at how much she had grown so quickly.

In that moment I realized that nothing other than breastmilk from me had ever entered her system. All of her twenty-seven inches and sixteen pounds (yes, she was an enormous five month old) had grown from what I had provided. All of her had come from all of me, not only her sustenance, but also her genetics (with a little of Nathan's mixed in, of course). She was truly made in my likeness.

Read

So God created mankind in his own image, in the image of God he created them; male and female he created them. God blessed them and said to them, "Be fruitful and increase in number; fill the earth and subdue it. Rule over the fish in the sea and the birds in the sky and over every living creature that moves on the ground." Then God said, "I give you every seed-bearing plant on the face of the whole earth and every tree that has fruit with seed in it. They will be yours for food. And to all the beasts of the earth and all the birds in the sky and all the creatures that move along the ground—everything that has

*the breath of life in it—I give every green plant for food." And it was so. God saw
all that he had made, and it was very good.*
—Genesis 1:27–31 NIV

Apply In the same way that all of five-month-old Everly came from me, all that we see in creation came from the mouth of God. He spoke everything into existence, and it is all good—especially humans, which he made in his own likeness, the very image of God. He sees us as very good. And yet, many times we find ourselves not valuing his creation with the honor and dignity that it deserves.

Even the best of us seem to find ways to undervalue people created in his image based on race, religion, political views, parenting methods, social media posts, and driving habits, to list a few. We have a responsibility as image-bearers of Christ to make sure that we never allow ourselves to rationalize the dehumanization of any group or individual. There is nothing that can separate a person from the love of Christ, and therefore we are called to love everyone in turn.

Pray Father, thank you for creating me in your image and giving me a responsibility to care for the rest of your creation. Reveal any prejudices that I may carry against my fellow image bearers, and give me eyes to see them in the same way that you do.

Reflect Who, as God's handiwork, do I undervalue?

_____

_____

Day Seventy

Mommy Hold You!

When Maya first met baby Everly, she didn't have issues with jealousy. She loved her baby sister! Interestingly enough, it took about four months for her to realize that this baby was getting in the way of Mommy's undivided attention. Combining this realization with the usual frustrations that arise from being two years old, Maya started having a lot of tantrums.

One day, I was getting the girls out of the car to go into a store. I had Everly in her car seat on one arm and was holding Maya's hand with the other.

"Mommy hold you!" Maya cried.

"Maya, I can't hold you right now. I have to hold Everly, because she can't walk. But you can, so you have to walk."

Maya chose this moment to melt down, right in the parking lot. Stomping, hopping, falling on the ground, flailing around, and screaming—the whole nine yards. As much as I dislike dealing with these tantrum moments, I understood her feelings. How often do I see God working in someone else's life and have a jealous little hissy fit because he isn't handling a situation in my life?

Read

Are not two sparrows sold for a penny? Yet not one of them will fall to the ground outside your Father's care. And even the very

hairs of your head are all numbered. So don't be afraid; you are worth more than
many sparrows.

—*Matthew 10:29–31 NIV*

Apply So many times, just like Maya, we would be perfectly
fine with our circumstances if we didn't look around
to make sure that they were just the same as everyone else's. We
tend to look at someone else being financially provided for, or
miraculously healed, or given the perfect child. We look at our own
struggles and wonder why God isn't caring for us in the same way.
Just as Maya doesn't understand that Everly has no choice but to be
carried, we don't know the particulars of any of the other situations
that we compare ourselves to. That is why this thought process is so
damaging.

Unlike us as moms, God does not have only two hands. He
doesn't have to put one of his children down in order to pick up
another. His attention for each of us is undivided and infinitely loving.
He cares for us more than we can imagine, and his plans for us are
good. There will be moments when we feel abandoned and cry out,
"Father, hold me!" The truth is that he is right by our side, and he
has never let us go.

Pray Father, protect my heart and mind from the desire to
compare my journey and relationship with you to that
of others. Thank you for the promise that you will never leave me or
forsake me and that you have good plans for my life.

Reflect List some ways in which God has been gracious:

Day
Seventy
One

I Probably Just Crawl

One of the hardest lessons for Maya to learn has been to come when called. Whether it's to change a diaper, get dressed, get in the car, or come to dinner, when it is time to come, she consistently runs the other direction. She is learning slowly that if she does not obey immediately, there will be a consequence. The other night when I told her to go to her room so that we could put on pajamas, I could see her little mind weighing the options.

"Maya, if you don't walk to your room, I'm going to pick you up and take you there."

"No carry me!" she cried.

"Then you need to walk."

She considered for one more moment, "I probably just crawl." With that she got down on all fours and crawled slowly at sloth speed to her bedroom, the whole way saying things like, "I going *right now*, Mommy," and "I do what you say."

I couldn't help but roll my eyes. She simply had to push the boundaries just a little, even if it meant crawling to her room.

Read

You are my portion, Lord; I have promised to obey your words. I have sought your face with all my heart; be gracious to me according to your promise. I have considered my ways and have turned my steps to your statutes. I will hasten and not delay to obey your commands.

—Psalm 119:57–60 NIV

Apply A mom knows that reluctant or half-hearted obedience, while following the letter of the law, is not the same as joyful, whole-hearted obedience. Instead, it is frustrating. It is essentially an act of defiance that shows respect for the consequence, rather than respect for the authority enforcing the boundary. It is the same in our relationship with God.

His desire is not for us to grudgingly submit to his laws out of fear of punishment, but to delight in obeying him out of trust that the boundaries he sets are for our benefit and protection. In the same way that we make rules for the protection and well-being of our children, God gives us boundaries because he loves us. We show him our gratitude and trust when we are quick and intentional in our obedience.

Pray Father, I apologize for the times that I have grudgingly obeyed you out a sense of obligation rather than trusting you to have my best interests in mind. Continue to convict me in these situations so that I can become more like Christ in my daily life. Thank you for placing boundaries in my life that are meant for my protection.

Reflect In what area do I need to delight in obeying God rather than simply obeying out of obligation?

Day
Seventy
Two

Heavy Burdens

Maya went through a phase in which anytime we would leave the house, she would gather things as she went to take with her. It would be anything that happened to be in her path—a stuffed animal, a sippy cup, a single shoe, her hairbrush, etc. We eventually had to come up with a rule that she could only walk out the door with one thing.

One day before the "one thing" rule was enacted, we were getting ready to go for a walk. Maya gathered up as many stuffed animals as she could carry. Walking out the door, she had five animals wrapped in her little arms—a monkey, a giraffe, a turtle, a sheep, and a baby doll. I told her that whatever she decided to bring, she would have to carry by herself. She agreed. We walked on the sidewalk and got seven houses down when she stopped.

"Are you tired?" I asked. Without answering, she laid down on her back in the middle of the sidewalk, arms still stretched around the animals. I stood awkwardly next to her as cars passed giving us strange looks, and a jogger went in the grass to get around us. We stayed there a good five minutes before she decided to get up and return home.

Read   *"Come to me, all you who are weary and burdened, and I will give you rest. Take my yoke upon you and learn from me, for I am gentle and humble in heart, and you will find rest for your souls. For my yoke is easy and my burden is light."*

- Matthew 11:28-30 NIV

Apply   On our journey through life we carry a lot of burdens, things that we think we need to hold on to and carry with us. However, the reality is that carrying all of this is tiring. It keeps us from finishing our journey and experiencing the full adventure that God has for us. While we love the idea of Christ taking away our burdens, many times when we have the opportunity to leave them at his feet, we opt for keeping them a little longer.

The problem is that in laying down our burdens, we are agreeing to take up the burden of Christ. We can refuse to do so for many reasons—fear of the unknown, pride in our own abilities, a sense of unworthiness, or an unwillingness to try a new way. While taking up the cross of Christ is not the natural action for our human nature, it will bring rest for our souls.

Pray   Father, help me to trust you with my burdens, releasing them fully to you as many times as is necessary to truly be free. Help me to overcome anything that stands in the way of me taking up the cross of Christ. Thank you for the rest that you promise for my soul.

Reflect   What burden do I need to relinquish today?

First Tear

By the grace of God, babies are born without the ability to produce tears. It is several weeks before their tear ducts begin working, which is wonderful because babies cry a lot. I still remember Maya's first tear like it was yesterday. We were driving in the car when she awoke from a nap in her car seat and started wailing, hungry for food and wanting it NOW! I was a flustered, hormonal, new mom, who lost all rational sense and logic while my baby was crying.

It took me a few minutes to pull over into a parking lot. I leapt from the car and opened the back door. There she was in her car seat with two huge tears rolling down her perfectly pink cheeks. I was not prepared for this. I am not a crier. It happens only on a rare occasion, or when I'm dicing onions. But seeing her tears, I cried. Silent tears streamed down my cheeks as I unclipped her from her car seat and held her close to my chest to comfort her before trying to feed her.

Read

The righteous cry out, and the Lord hears them; he delivers them from all their troubles. The Lord is close to the brokenhearted and saves those who are crushed in spirit.

—Psalm 34:17–18 NIV

Apply There is some hormonal change that happens when we become mothers that makes us attentive to the cries of our children in a way that we have never experienced before. Our hearts break with theirs, and it is the same with our Heavenly Father. God created a sinless world for us to share with him in perfect unity. However, with Adam and Eve's choice to sin, we developed the ability to shed tears as pain and death entered the picture.

The dark world that we live in today is not what God had planned for us, and yet when we experience pain, he does not use blame or say "I told you so." Instead, God weeps with us. He enters into our pain. He draws us close to him for comfort. He wraps us in his love and promises hope by giving us a new opportunity for unity with him through redemption in Christ.

Pray Father, thank you for your unending love by comforting me in my pain and for offering me another chance at unity with you through Jesus. Thank you for promising to hear when I call and to draw near in my pain.

Reflect What pain do I need to pour out before the Lord today?

_____

_____

_____

_____

Day Seventy Four

Preparing the Nursery

One of my favorite parts of being pregnant is preparing the nursery. For both of my daughters, I ordered fabric and sewed their nursery essentials. They each have a set of matching sheets, crib skirts, changing pad covers, curtains, throw pillows, blankets, and quilts. I searched for countless hours on the internet to pick out the perfect fabric for each of them and countless more hours sewing the different pieces in preparation for their arrival.

I am a planner, so I had the crib set up, the clothes folded and put in the dresser drawers, and the closet stocked with organized bins of baby essentials months before their due dates. I ordered custom artwork for the walls with their names and Bible verses that I prayed over them before they were born. I have such fond memories of those quiet moments in the empty nursery, dreaming of the day when my baby would share it with me.

Read   *My Father's house has many rooms; if that were not so, would I have told you that I am going there to prepare a place for you? And if I go and prepare a place for you, I will come back and take you to be with me that you also may be where I am. You know the way to the place where I am going."*

Thomas said to him, "Lord, we don't know where you are going, so how can we know the way?"

Jesus answered, "I am the way and the truth and the life. No one comes to the Father except through me.

—John 14:2–6 NIV

Apply Our Father in Heaven is preparing a place for us in this very moment. He is planning for our arrival with great anticipation. He is making personal touches to welcome us to our new home and is eagerly looking forward to the day when we will join him in the paradise he has completed for us. With the same love with which we look forward to our own children, he is waiting expectantly for us.

My babies could not comprehend the amazing world they would be born into, and there are no words to explain to us how incredible our arrival into Heaven will be. We can only trust that our Father has given great attention to every detail and is longing to share it with us! If we ever worry about how to reach our heavenly home, the verses make it clear that there is no ambiguity. The way is through Chirst alone.

Pray Father, thank you for the love and care that you put into preparing heaven for me! Help me to rest in the knowledge that reaching heaven will be a joyful moment of long-awaited reunion with you!

Reflect How does this view of Heaven change my perspective towards everyday life on earth?

Day Seventy Five

Distracted Eater

Everly has to be the most distracted eater ever born, which is pretty inconvenient considering that Maya is a very animated and distracting toddler. This week as I was trying to breastfeed Everly, the typical happened. Just as Everly started to eat, Maya bounded into the room and attempted to put sunglasses on Everly, who unlatched, causing milk to spew everywhere.

I tried to get Maya to leave the room creatively, "Maya, do you want to go color in your room?"

"No," she replied, squishing Everly's feet in her hands while Everly giggled and squealed, completely forgetting she was eating.

"Maya can you go play quietly while I feed Everly?"

"Ok," she sat down next to the chair, grabbed her play cupcakes, and dumped them all out, clattering across the tile floor. There's the end of that meal attempt. I'm pretty sure Everly won't finish a full feeding session ever again unless I lock the two of us into a completely dark room with soundproof walls.

Read

"And when you pray, do not be like the hypocrites, for they love to pray standing in the synagogues and on the street corners to be seen by others. Truly I tell you, they have received their reward in full. But when you pray, go into your room, close the door and pray to your Father, who is

unseen. Then your Father, who sees what is done in secret, will reward you. And when you pray, do not keep on babbling like pagans, for they think they will be heard because of their many words. Do not be like them, for your Father knows what you need before you ask him.

—Matthew 6:5–8 NIV

Apply Why is it that all the distractions seem to surface when we are trying to pray? I always assumed these verses were only about being secretive, but I think it's more than that. When we are praying out loud in public, our thoughts are distracted by those around us. What is everyone thinking about the prayer? Have I prayed long enough? Did I already say that? It is very difficult to stay focused on God when the room is full of people.

The best place to have some undistracted prayer time is closed up in a room by yourself with nothing else to do! We have to be intentional about blocking out the noise to make room to talk to God. This may mean waking up before the kids, leaving the cell phone in the other room, or writing prayers down to keep us on task and focused. Another big distraction pointed out in these verses is an abundance of words. Sometimes the words get in the way, and we need to simply sit still and be in God's presence. Don't worry, God doesn't need to hear all the words to know what we are saying.

Pray Father, thank you for the opportunity to come into your presence and talk with you. Help me to be able to focus on you during our time together and to block out the many distractions that get in the way of my being present in prayer.

Reflect Where can I go to have intentional, focused prayer time?

Day Seventy Six

Mesa Verde Dirt

We took a vacation to Colorado a few months after Maya learned how to walk. Everywhere she went, Maya was in major discovery mode. We went on a tour of a museum, and she circled up and down the handicap ramp over the stairs for half an hour. When touring the ruins at Mesa Verde, she discovered humidity-free dirt. While dirt in Louisiana clings to everything in the thick humidity, Colorado dirt is powdery, light, and dry. It puffs in a little cloud around your foot with each step.

Once Maya discovered this, in her mind, the tour was over. Right in front of our group of thirty people, she leaned over and put her hands in the dirt, rubbing them around. She plopped her bottom down in it and started wiggling her legs around until they were covered in a thin film. Soon she dove belly first into inches deep of dust, quite literally swimming in it, making a toddler version of a dirt angel. By this time in the vacation, I was so over trying to keep her on task and was just happy that she was occupying herself, to the great amusement of everyone on the tour. My response—she's already dirty, what is a little more going to hurt?

Read

What shall we say, then? Shall we go on sinning so that grace may increase? By no means! We are those who have died to sin; how can we live in it any longer? Or don't you know that all of us who were baptized into Christ Jesus were baptized into his death? We were therefore buried with him through baptism into death in order that, just as Christ was raised from the dead through the glory of the Father, we too may live a new life.

—Romans 6:1–4 NIV

Apply Sometimes, when we mess up or find ourselves caught in a cycle of sin, we tend to have the same opinion that I had about the dirt. Since we're already sinning, why not continue? Besides, we have such wonderful assurance of God's love and Christ's forgiveness, what's the point in trying to be perfect all the time? True, perfection is impossible and should never be our goal for its own sake. However, when we consider the lengths that Jesus went to in order to offer us this unending forgiveness, how could we ever take it lightly or for granted?

You see, we know when it's time to end our dirty acts, but it can be so easy and tempting to just keep going in the same direction. However, forgiveness is granted not on technicalities, but on the posture of our hearts. We must repent, which literally means "to turn around," in order to be forgiven. If our hearts have not truly turned away from our sin, then they cannot turn to Jesus.

Pray Father, thank you for your promise to love me and forgive me no matter what I have done. Help me to not take advantage of that assurance and use it as an excuse to continue in sin.

Reflect How have I taken Christ's forgiveness for granted?

Feeding Everly

I have discovered that the only thing messier than Maya eating, is Maya feeding her baby sister, Everly. For months, we trained Maya that she could not put anything into Everly's mouth. Now that Everly is eating baby food, Maya is all about being a helpful big sister and being the one to feed her at meal times.

After lots of training on how to only put a little on the spoon, to wait until Everly opens her mouth, to put only the tip of the spoon in and not shove the whole thing down her throat, Maya has definitely improved, but that is not saying much. Within minutes, the table is covered in smeared, pureed carrots, the orange goop dripping down Everly's chin onto her clothes. Maya's hands, the spoon, and the table are a sticky mess. Feeding Everly is a messy job, but someone has to do it, no matter how unqualified.

Read

Jesus called his twelve disciples to him and gave them authority to drive out impure spirits and to heal every disease and sickness. These twelve Jesus sent out with the following instructions: "Do not go among the Gentiles or enter any town of the Samaritans. Go rather to the lost sheep of Israel. As you go, proclaim this message: 'The kingdom of heaven has come near.' Heal the sick, raise the dead, cleanse those who have leprosy, drive out demons. Freely you have received; freely give.

—Matthew 10:1, 5–8 NIV

Apply In the same way that I give Maya the authority to feed Everly, as seemingly unfit for the job as she is, Jesus has given us a commission to tell others about him. If we feel overwhelmed by the task and completely intimidated, fearing that we aren't the best candidates, it's because that's absolutely the case. In these verses, Jesus calls his twelve disciples, who are fishermen and tax collectors by trade, to drive out demons and heal the sick. Talk about giving a big responsibility to a group pretty much guaranteed to fail!

In the same way, the task God has placed before us is way above our pay grade. We are bound to make a mess of it, and yet, he has not chosen us incorrectly. He promises to give us the words to say, the defense that we need in the face of opposition, and the wisdom to know the right actions to take. Sharing Christ with others is an important job, and while we will make a mess of it at times, we are the ones he has entrusted with the responsibility.

Pray Father, thank you for giving me the opportunity to be a part of your story, for giving me a purpose in sharing the truth with others. Give me the courage to speak up and be an example for you even when it is overwhelming and even when I feel intimidated, knowing that you are with me.

Reflect How has God used a mess that I've made for good, in spite of my best efforts?

Day
Seventy
Eight

Burping

When Maya was a baby she had pretty severe reflux. Air bubbles trapped while eating would cause her excruciating pain, and she would cry non-stop. The only thing we could do was try to burp her constantly. At the height of her reflux, she would wake up screaming in pain usually every hour or so through the night needing to be burped.

It was so frustrating as a mother that something so small could cause such harm and pain to my little baby. Getting all of her air bubbles out through constant burping was exhausting, tedious work. In that season, I was a frazzled mess from lack of sleep. I never thought that I would find myself praying so fervently for burps! Eventually, after about six weeks or so, we got on the other side of the reflux, and it was such a relief!

Read   *Therefore, rid yourselves of all malice and all deceit, hypocrisy, envy, and slander of every kind. Like newborn babies, crave pure spiritual milk, so that by it you may grow up in your salvation, now that you have tasted that the Lord is good.*

—1 Peter 2:1–3 NIV

Apply It is amazing what a small amount of sin in our lives can cause vast amounts of pain. In order to live a life of freedom from the consequences of sin, we must do the exhausting and tedious work of getting rid of every shred of sin in our lives, identifying and removing it one piece at a time.

If we digest the pure, spiritual milk of God's Word, but allow any false teaching or selfish interpretations of scripture to leak in, we will be faced with the more difficult work of purging it out. We must be careful what we incorporate into our beliefs, how we act upon those beliefs, and what sins we have the temptation to excuse as insignificant in our walk with Christ. But there is hope—on the other side of the conscientious task of working out our salvation is the blessing of living in the Lord's goodness!

Pray Father, please expose any sin and convict my heart so that I can eagerly take part in ridding it from my life. Give me the perseverance to continue rooting out these sins so that I can experience the fullness of freedom that you have planned for me.

Reflect What small sin is causing great pain in my life today?

_____

_____

_____

_____

_____

_____

Cleaning with Soap

From the way that Maya loves to clean things, one would think that I must set a great example of cleaning as her mother. I'll let people keep thinking that. The other day while I was trying to rock Everly to sleep for nap, Maya found a piece of soap in the shower and proceeded to clean everything—the floor, the counters, herself, the furniture, the rug, etc.

While she did a very thorough job, the end result was a layer of white soap streaks all over everything. She had such good intentions of being helpful, when in reality, I had to go behind her and scrub the dried soap film off of everything during her nap time. Her cleaning job had made quite a mess!

Read

"Woe to you, teachers of the law and Pharisees, you hypocrites! You clean the outside of the cup and dish, but inside they are full of greed and self-indulgence. Blind Pharisee! First clean the inside of the cup and dish, and then the outside also will be clean. "Woe to you, teachers of the law and Pharisees, you hypocrites! You are like whitewashed tombs, which look beautiful on the outside but on the inside are full of the bones of the dead and everything unclean. In the same way, on the outside you appear to people as righteous but on the inside you are full of hypocrisy and wickedness.

—Matthew 23:25–28 NIV

Apply   In the same way that Maya was trying to be helpful, the Pharisees had good intentions in cleaning up the outside of their lives, and we do too. We think that if we look good on the outside, like we have it all together, then others will see our lives and want the Jesus that we have. The problem is that we portray a false image of Jesus, a Jesus that we don't really need because we have already saved ourselves. This false portrayal is not the Jesus who loves us and died for us or the one that others will desire.

When we cover the reality of our struggles to others, it is like rubbing ourselves down with soap, creating even more of a mess than before. We leave Christ with the difficult work of slowly cleaning off the waxy film of deceit and hypocrisy that we are covered in. As vulnerable as it may feel, we are called to be honest, raw, open, and sincere with those around us. The truth is that we are not naturally beautiful, and we need a Savior working to recreate us from the inside out every day. *That* is the Jesus that the world is waiting to see at work in us!

Pray   Father, thank you for making my need for a Savior so clear! Help me to live my life with sincerity, representing myself in an honest and open light with others, admitting in humility that I need saving.

Reflect   How do I represent myself to others differently from reality?

Cloth Diapers

I use cloth diapers, and I love them. Yep, I'm that mom. My reasons for cloth diapering are as follows: 1) they save me *so* much money, 2) they save the environment from mountains of diapers that won't break down until Jesus returns, 3) I am really thrifty and don't like to spend money on something that holds poop, 4) they are so cute and fluffy, and 5) disposables are expensive.

So obviously, you can tell that the future of the world and caring for the environment are my top priorities in this decision, and not the money. Seriously though, it takes a disposable diaper five hundred years to decompose. It just doesn't make sense to me to use something that would still be sitting around full of poop fifteen generations after I am gone.

Read

"You shall not make for yourself an image in the form of anything in heaven above or on the earth beneath or in the waters below. You shall not bow down to them or worship them; for I, the Lord your God, am a jealous God, punishing the children for the sin of the parents to the third and fourth generation of those who hate me, but showing love to a thousand generations of those who love me and keep my commandments.

—Exodus 20:4–6 NIV

Apply   There are plenty of legacies that I want to leave
behind for future generations, and while a landfill full
of diapers isn't on the list, it isn't the worst burden that I could pass
on to my children. Our actions as moms create an environment in our
homes that our kids soak up like sponges. The lifestyle that we lead
day to day influences them in so many intangible ways. We pass
down generational blessings and curses without even being aware of
them.

Most generational curses begin with misplaced worship,
whether it is an addiction, an obsessive hobby, or time-consuming
activities. Any time we center our lives around anything other than
Christ, we are giving in to idolatry. However, when we follow God
wholeheartedly, we leave blessings for thousands of generations to
follow! That is something worth leaving behind!

Pray   Father, reveal to me anything in my life that is taking
the first place that you rightly deserve. Give me the
strength to set it aside and return to wholeheartedly worship you.
Thank you for the promise that you will carry my devotion on as a
blessing to my family for generations to come.

Reflect   What legacy do I want to pass on to my children?

_____

_____

_____

_____

Day Eighty One

Sleeping Through the Night

I made a choice last night, and I realize that I chose temporary comfort over long-term peace, but at the time, I didn't care. Here's what happened: Everly woke up crying at two o'clock in the morning. She has been sleeping through the night pretty well, but for the last week or so she keeps waking up and wanting to eat at two.

The pediatrician warned me that this would happen and told me to rock her back to sleep without feeding her. Otherwise, she will get into the habit of waking up to eat in the night. Here's the thing—if I let her cry, she will wake up Maya, and then I have two kids awake. If I rock her back to sleep, she'll wake up again to eat later.

Last night, I realized something—if I feed her now, she will sleep until morning. If I don't, she will be waking me up again in a few hours. I theoretically know the long-term consequences of this decision, that she may decide to wake up every night to eat from now on. But I was tired. And I fed her. And I got some sleep. And it was wonderful.

Read

Once when Jacob was cooking some stew, Esau came in from the open country, famished. He said to Jacob, "Quick, let me have some of that red stew! I'm famished!"

Jacob replied, "First sell me your birthright." "Look, I am about to die,"

Esau said. "What good is the birthright to me?" But Jacob said, "Swear to me first." So he swore an oath to him, selling his birthright to Jacob. Then Jacob gave Esau some bread and some lentil stew. He ate and drank, and then got up and left. So Esau despised his birthright.

—Genesis 25:29-30a, 31–34 NIV

Apply I think, as a mom, that I am just now understanding this story. I used to wonder, how could someone trade their birthright for a bowl of soup? But moms totally understand how we can be so tired, or so hungry, that we would be willing to trade the eternal for just five minutes of relief. In some cases, like our baby's sleep schedule, the consequences aren't lasting. Eventually, Everly will sleep through the night.

However, there are eternal things that we trade for temporary comfort that do have a lasting impact on our lives and the lives of those around us. It could be choosing to scroll mindlessly on our phone in those quiet five minutes rather than opening the Bible app. It could be to give in to a little gossip rather than walking away or changing the subject. It could be letting thoughts of jealousy, pride, or inadequacy consume us rather than pursuing God's truth. Each time we choose our own way instead of God's, we allow habits of disobedience to thrive in our lives which cause us to value the temporary over the eternal. It happens one decision at a time.

Pray Father, I'm sorry for the many ways that I choose the temporary over the eternal every day. Convict me and give me the discipline to make the decision to actively choose you.

Reflect In what ways do I choose the temporary?

Mother's Day Out Magic

Right before she turned two-and-a-half, Maya started attending Mother's Day Out. This is the Best. Thing. Ever. Until that point, it had been me and Maya, and later Everly as well, all day, every day, all the time. I love spending so much time with my girls, but Maya tends to start tuning me out since I am the voice narrating ninety percent of her world.

After Mother's Day Out, I started to notice some great things happening—she was less attached to her pacifier, she started saying "yes, ma'am," and she started sharing toys and learning how to play well with other kids. All of these are things that I had tried to teach her, but she did not learn from me. I can't begin to explain what a relief it was to have another partner in the process of raising our headstrong little girl. Let's face it, training children in the way they should go is hard work!

Read   *Two are better than one, because they have a good return for their labor: If either of them falls down, one can help the other up. But pity anyone who falls and has no one to help them up. Also, if two lie down together, they will keep warm. But how can one keep warm alone? Though one may be overpowered, two can defend themselves. A cord of three strands is not quickly broken.*

—Ecclesiastes 4:9–12 NIV

Apply   You know who else benefits from more than one positive influence as they grow? Us! In the same way that another voice echoing my instructions to Maya solidified it to her, we must allow Christian mentors who are strong in their faith to come alongside us and pour into our lives. It is amazing how a fellow mom, leader, or friend can echo the lessons that God is teaching us in our personal time of study, reinforcing them in our lives.

In turn, we should also be in the process of helping those who are one step behind us in their spiritual journey by offering encouragement and wisdom. We must be careful and prayerful when selecting these mentors and mentees, though. These will be the voices that shape the reasoning behind our decisions, help hold us accountable when we wander, and shine the light into our darkest seasons. If we want to shore up our spiritually-weak points, we must do it in community!

Pray   Father, help me to find trustworthy individuals who have a heart after you with whom I can walk through life. Thank you for giving me good examples of community in the Bible that I can follow. Help me to be vulnerable and honest with these individuals so that I can continue to grow.

Reflect   Who do I allow to speak into my life? Who am I mentoring in turn?

_____

_____

_____

Day Eighty Three

Due Date Unknown

With Maya, I was induced, and she was born ten days after her due date. In light of that, the doctor pushed my due date with Everly back by ten days. Still, she waited another week after that before making her arrival. Every morning, I would wonder—will it be today? No. I wanted the house to be clean when we got home from the hospital, so every day I would clean the house, run the dishwasher and empty it, and wash the laundry so that everything would be done at any given time.

Each night going to bed, I would ask myself—will it be tonight? Still no. Each night before bed I would make sure the car was packed with our bags for the hospital, our family members who would be keeping Maya kept their cell phones on, and we had our clothes laid out and ready for the inevitable arrival of our baby.

But the days continued to slip by. I found myself bringing a meal to a friend of mine whose baby had been due a week after mine. She was now home from the hospital with her bundle of joy, while I was still waddling around like a beached whale. I definitely resonated with the use of the term 'expecting' for being pregnant in those last days of waiting. Everly's imminent arrival was all that I could think about.

Read Heaven and earth will pass away, but my words will never pass away. "But about that day or hour no one knows, not even the angels in heaven, nor the Son, but only the Father. Be on guard! Be alert! You do not know when that time will come."

—Mark 13:31–33 NIV

Apply We know that Jesus is coming back, and that it will be the event of all eternity. The Bible teaches us to be on our guard, to wait expectantly, to prepare our hearts, and to live our lives in such a way that we are ready for it to happen at any given moment. However, as the years, decades, and generations slip by, it is easy to understand why we struggle to live with a sense of expectancy for Christ's return.

In the same way that I lived my life differently as my due date approached, there are many ways that we would live our lives differently if we viewed each day as if it were our last. How would we clean and prepare our hearts? How would we alert those around us? How would we spend our time and energy? Let's start each morning with a glimpse of eternity in our hearts.

Pray Father, thank you for the promise that Jesus will return triumphantly one day. Help me to live each day with the end in mind, and to eagerly await that reunion with a prepared heart.

Reflect How would my everyday life look different if I lived with a sense of expectancy for Christ's return?

Hearing Loss

Sometimes I think Maya may be suffering from early onset hearing loss (it may run in the family, because Nathan has a similar problem.) I start to wonder when we have this conversation:

"Mommy, I can eat this on the sofa?" she asks holding up her peanut butter and jelly sandwich.

"No, you have to eat your sandwich in the kitchen."

"But I can eat it in the den?" she asks expectantly.

"No," I reply, "Food is messy, so we eat it in the kitchen."

"I probably just eat it on the rug and sit," she comes up with a perfectly logical solution in her mind.

"No," I repeat, "If you leave the table, that means you are finished eating, and the food stays here."

"Ok," she nods, as though I'm being reasonable, "I go in the den with my food now."

Are we speaking two different languages? How many ways can I tell her no?

Read

Do not merely listen to the word, and so deceive yourselves. Do what it says. Anyone who listens to the word but does not do what it says is like someone who looks at his face in a mirror and, after looking at himself, goes away and immediately forgets what he looks like. But whoever looks

intently into the perfect law that gives freedom, and continues in it—not forgetting
what they have heard, but doing it—they will be blessed in what they do.
—James 1:22–25 NIV

Apply   Maya hears what she wants to hear rather than what I am actually saying, and we tend to do the same thing with God's Word. We read our Bibles and nod our heads and agree with everything we are learning. Then we walk out the door and have a tendency to do exactly what we had already decided we were going to do, regardless of the truth. Other times, we use the instruction that God meant for us as a weapon to wield against others, twisting the words to suit our own desires.

We read about loving others but post scathing remarks on Facebook about someone different from us. We learn about generosity but write our tithe checks grudgingly. We know to put others first but see everything in our world through the lens of how it affects us. While we cling to God's promises, it is easy to forget that many of those promises come with a prerequisite of following him in ways that we would rather overlook. While it is difficult, we need to take a long, hard look in the mirror and not give excuses for what is reflected.

Pray   Father, I'm sorry for the ways that I read your Word and then continue to act in a way that is in opposition with your commands. Allow me to look honestly at my actions and show me the areas that do not correspond with the Bible.

Reflect   In what ways do I know the truth but live otherwise?

Labor of Love

Every birth story is different, but I wanted to give birth without any interventions if possible. To prepare for the big event, Nathan and I took Lamaze classes. One of the things that we learned in our classes is that in order to cope with the pain, I should focus on the reward at the end—which is, of course, the baby. I had to acknowledge that I was going through pain in order to accomplish an incredible task—birthing a new human being into the world!

You see, as a pregnant woman, I was not looking forward to the pain of labor. I had plenty of doubts about my ability to accomplish the task before me. I knew that there would be pain, and that it would be almost more than I could bear. However, one thought would help me push through to the end—the anticipation of meeting our daughter, of holding her in my arms, of gazing into the eyes of that precious face, and beginning a relationship with her in her new life! That reward made all of the pain pale in comparison.

Read

After Jesus said this, he looked toward heaven and prayed: "Father, the hour has come. Glorify your Son, that your Son may glorify you. For you granted him authority over all people that he might give eternal life to all those you have given him. Now this is eternal life: that they know you, the only true God, and Jesus Christ, whom you have sent. —John 17:1-3 NIV

Apply In the same way that I focused on my baby as a reward, when Jesus died on the cross, he had one thought on his mind that allowed him to complete his task. That thought was ME! It was YOU! He so desired a personal relationship with us and the opportunity to bring about new life that he literally faced hell in order to give us that chance.

He was thinking of us in the moment where he reached the end of himself, and love was all that could sustain him—love for a sinful, undeserving people. I don't know why Jesus' death had to be so painful, but the thought of it is overwhelming and incredibly humbling for me. I feel so loved! So cherished! And so undeserving. We truly are his children. He has birthed us in his blood! And at the end of it all, he considered us a reward that made the pain pale in comparison.

Pray Father, thank you for giving your Son, Jesus, to die for me! Thank you for loving me so much and finding me valuable enough to allow such sacrifice. Help me to never diminish the incredible truth that I am sought after and cherished by you!

Reflect How does Jesus' attitude toward the pain of his sacrifice make me feel?

_____

_____

_____

_____

_____

Find Your Happy Place

When I was preparing to give birth, I knew that pain was going to be involved. I did not know the exact hour, but I knew that this pain would have to happen in order to bring my baby into the world. While anticipating the pain was stressful, it also gave me time and motivation to prepare.

In our birthing classes, we practiced several pain management techniques. I typed out a description of my happy place and had Nathan read it out loud while I worked on mental visualization of that place and doing deep breathing. We practiced visiting this happy place so many times that when the real contractions began, I was already in the habit of putting my mind over matter and focusing on the happy place in the midst of the pain.

Read

[Jesus] withdrew about a stone's throw beyond them, knelt down and prayed, "Father, if you are willing, take this cup from me; yet not my will, but yours be done." An angel from heaven appeared to him and strengthened him. And being in anguish, he prayed more earnestly, and his sweat was like drops of blood falling to the ground.

—Luke 22:41–44 NIV

Apply Jesus' pain on the cross was also anticipated. He knew in advance the kind of pain, both physical and emotional, that he would have to endure in order to complete his task. In fact, the thought of the pain filled him with so much anxiety that he even prayed to God that there would be another way, any other way, to take away the pain and still finish the job. But it was not possible. He was so distressed that his sweat came out as blood! This makes me feel a little better about my own anxiety.

In the same way that I practiced going to my happy place, Jesus prepared to face his imminent pain through fervent prayer and intimate communion with the Father. Jesus' consistent practice of taking time to talk to the Father in prayer throughout his life gave him the ability to retreat to that same safe connection while he was enduring the pain of the cross. The habit of prayer Jesus had put into place was the natural reaction for him when his limits were challenged. If we practice the same habit of seeking God in the everyday, then turning to him in the challenges will be a natural reaction.

Pray Father, help me to spend time preparing for the pain of this life by being intimately connected with you in all seasons. Thank you for being present in my life and meeting with me when I come to you in prayer.

Reflect How can I prepare for the pain that I will face in life?

_____

_____

Mommy, Mommy, Mommy!

Maya is at the phase where she says, "Mommy, Mommy, Mommy, Mommy!" constantly.

And I try telling her, "I am literally right here, holding you in my arms, you do not have to keep calling my name." I think that if I hear it one more time, I'll lose my mind.

But when that sweet girl goes down for her nap, I literally cannot wait to hear her little voice when she wakes up saying, "Mommy, where are you?"

Another new favorite phrase of hers is "No, Mommy!" On those days, Maya is more independent and doesn't want me to hold her, hug her, and smother her with kisses. On those days, I let her do her thing, but when she eventually needs some help and calls my name, I am there to answer no matter how long she has avoided me. I love her the same no matter what kind of day she is having. What could she do to make me not love her?

Read

They will call on my name and I will answer them; I will say, 'They are my people,' and they will say, 'The Lord is our God.'"
—*Zechariah 13:9 NIV*

And everyone who calls on the name of the Lord will be saved.' —*Acts 2:21 NIV*

Apply I don't know about you, but when I truly think about it, Christ's love for us is pretty intimidating. With all that he went through for us, it should make us want to spend time with him above all else, but instead we get distracted. By really worthless things. Things like social media, shopping online during naptime, or scrolling, just mindlessly scrolling on our phones.

When we stop to think about about how we have given up precious time with the one who created us and loves us in exchange for negative habits and attitudes, we feel disgusted with ourselves! We think that there is no way that we could possibly do enough to show God that we're serious about seeking him this time. I mean, after Jesus' big gesture on the cross, what could we possibly give to make up for all of our worthless wanderings and distractions?

Here is the great news—God doesn't need or want a big gesture. He just wants to spend time with us. We know how unconditionally we love our own kids, so how much more must God love us? When we find it difficult to keep up spending quality time with God, he hasn't given us a mountain to climb to get back to him. All we have to do is say his name—he can't wait to hear it!

Pray Father, turn my heart to you! Help me to value my time with you above anything else. Instead of giving in to feeling guilty when I get distracted, allow me to run unhindered back into your arms.

Reflect What distraction do I need to actively set aside to create more time to be with God?

Creature of Habit

Maya is a creature of habit. She thrives in an environment with predictable schedules, rules, and consequences. Even in things that are her choice, such as which toys to play with at certain times, she is usually pretty predictable. She always likes to read books in the evenings, play outside after TV time, do puzzles before nap, etc.

When something in Maya's world changes without warning, it definitely throws her off. For example, she gets TV time at the same time every day, right after she wakes up from nap. (This works well because she wakes up really cranky.) One Saturday morning while I was running errands, Nathan let her watch TV after breakfast. For the next week, she asked me every morning for TV time. Another example is one day when Nathan was not going to work because it was a weekend.

Maya said, "No, Daddy. You have to go to work. You can come home at dinner time."

Read *Then the Lord said: "I am making a covenant with you. Before all your people I will do wonders never before done in any nation in all the world. The people you live among will see how awesome is the work that I, the Lord, will do for you.*

—Exodus 34:10 NIV

Apply   Just like Maya, we like to be in the know about what is going on. Wouldn't it be lovely for God to let us in on his will and show us what is coming next? Instead, we worship a mysterious and creative God who never works his wonders in the same way twice. Sometimes he doesn't reveal what he has in store because it is so overwhelming that we would back away in intimidation, never thinking it possible.

Other times, he keeps his ways secret because he knows that the opposite would happen. If we knew his plans, we would rush ahead and mess everything up by not waiting for his timing. We also might somehow try to take credit for the work that he is doing. God loves to lead us in such a way that we have to be dependent on him. He has incredible plans for our lives, and he can't wait to show us what they are, all in due time.

Pray   Father, thank you for having good plans for me, plans so incredible that I never could have imagined them! Give me the patience to wait for your timing, to depend on you in all things, and to give you the glory when your wonders begin.

Reflect What unbelievable wonders has God done in my life?

_____

_____

_____

_____

Day Eighty Nine

Loud Mouth

Everly is a very quiet baby. Ninety percent of the time, she doesn't make a single peep, content to just watch the action around her. However, when she does decide to open her mouth, she is LOUD. She really has two volumes—off and full blast! It is so unexpected that it takes people off guard. If someone is holding her head close to their ear when she decides to let loose, it can be fairly deafening.

Unlike what one would expect, almost all of these loud outbursts are ones of pure joy. A video of her full body laughter could totally go viral on social media. It is that intense. Her happy squeals and gurgles come out sounding more like a wraith screeching than a baby laughing. However, these sounds are the uninhibited expression of a contagiously joyful spirit.

Read

My dear brothers and sisters, take note of this: Everyone should be quick to listen, slow to speak and slow to become angry.

—James 1:19 NIV

Rejoice in the Lord always. I will say it again: Rejoice!

—Philippians 4:4 NIV

He will yet fill your mouth with laughter and your lips with shouts of joy.

—Job 8:21 NIV

Apply Everly is a great example of how we should speak as Christians. We need to have two modes—listening (and not speaking) or spreading the joy without limit. Our words should be few, well-thought out, and tempered. The Bible teaches over and over that having wisdom and thinking before speaking go hand-in-hand. Words, though intangible, matter deeply. They can cause life or death in those who hear them. Before we speak, we must make sure that we are speaking life-giving truth.

It can be easy to take this idea to the extreme and believe that we should never speak up about what we believe for fear that someone may be offended. But our mouths were created for a purpose—to give glory to God. When it comes to praising him, our words should become shouts of joy! We can scream his goodness from the rooftops and not care who is listening. We don't need to suppress the overwhelming gladness we receive from God but can rejoice loudly in it!

Pray Father, thank you for the ways that you fill my life with joy! Let the words that come out of my mouth be an expression of joy overflowing into the lives of others.

Reflect How can I express uninhibited joy in Christ today?

_____

_____

_____

_____

Day Ninety

She Peed in the Cup!

Warning—this story talks at length about bodily functions, but you're a mom, so you can handle it. When Maya was fourteen months old, she had a mysterious fever of 100.6 degrees for a week. All of the tests came back negative. The pediatrician said that the next step was to test a urine sample for a urinary tract infection. This is a simple procedure for adults, but getting an infant to pee in a cup is complicated. The pediatrician suggested we use a catheter.

Nathan was out of town for work, and I was stressing out as only a new mother can. I convinced the pediatrician to give me a sample cup to take home for the day to see if I could get Maya to pee in it. She agreed that I could try and come back to do the catheter at the end of the day. I attempted all the things—had her stand in warm water, gave her lots of fluids, and kept her diaper off in case she went. Nothing worked. I prayed all day, quite fervently, that somehow she would pee in the cup, but it didn't happen.

We finally went back to the pediatrician, and I tried to be brave as they got Maya ready. One nurse was holding her down and the other was literally reaching to insert the catheter when Maya started peeing. Not a little bit, but a streaming arch into the air. I grabbed the cup, which I still had in my pocket, and caught the pee in it. I couldn't believe it! She peed in the cup!

Read

Do not be anxious about anything, but in every situation, by prayer and petition, with thanksgiving, present your requests to God. And the peace of God, which transcends all understanding, will guard your hearts and your minds in Christ Jesus.

—*Philippians 4:6–7 NIV*

Apply

Sometimes we worry about the most random things. They almost seem too strange to pray about. Will God be offended that I am asking him to get my daughter to pee in a cup? These verses make it clear which things we should pray about—anything that worries us. If that is peeing in a cup, then it qualifies!

While sometimes God answers in miraculous ways and just in time, this isn't always the case. Sometimes God gives us his peace instead, which brings inexplicable comfort in a way that only God can. No matter how small, insignificant, or strange our requests are, God is waiting to hear them. He knows what is bothering us, but he has set us free from the need to carry those burdens. We must lay them down, and lay them all down, so that he can guard our hearts and minds from slipping into worry.

Pray

Father, help me to not give in to worry but to lay all of my requests at your feet, no matter how small. Thank you for promising your peace in all situations.

Reflect

What worry do I need to lay down before God in prayer today?

Day
Ninety
One

I Just Have To Fix It

Maya loves to fix things. Maybe it is because we do a lot of DIY construction projects around the house, but she loves tools and constantly goes around trying to fix and build things. This week, she was playing with the remote that goes to the fan and light fixture in our bedroom. Knowing that Maya has a tendency to hide things and then forget where she put them, I asked her what she was doing with the remote.

"I just have to fix it," she replied.

She took the remote and used the buttons to turn on and off the lights and make the fan go fast and then slow. I got distracted by Everly needing a diaper change, and that night at bedtime, I realized that the remote was gone. We could still use the light switch to turn the light and fan on and off together, but not separately.

Nathan and I finally put our heads together and came up with a brilliant solution. We turned on the light switch and then unscrewed all of the light bulbs so that the lights were off and the fan was on. The bulbs were hot, so Nathan had to wear a sock on his hand. Then in the morning, we screwed all of the bulbs back in again. We have yet to find the remote, so this unique ritual still happens every morning and night. I can already tell we aren't going to be able to keep up this temporary fix forever.

Read For it is by grace you have been saved, through faith—and this is not from yourselves, it is the gift of God— not by works, so that no one can boast. For we are God's handiwork, created in Christ Jesus to do good works, which God prepared in advance for us to do.

—*Ephesians 2:8-10 NIV*

Apply Maya, in trying to fix our light fixture, created quite a hassle. The same thing can happen in our own lives. Sometimes we look at the sin in our lives and think, "I just have to fix it." The problem is that we can't fix it, and the more we try, the worse we make the situation. We can only be saved by God's grace, a free gift that he offers us through faith, our belief that Jesus is Lord. Nathan and I now actually have to fix our light every night and morning because of Maya's intervention. Similarly, we will have to keep working if we are trying to save ourselves by our actions.

As Christians, we fall into this performance trap all the time. Maybe it is trying to stop a sin without taking the time to confess it and ask God for help. Maybe it is trying to earn points by being really good or doing all of the right things. Maybe it consists of putting on a front that looks like we don't have any issues needing forgiveness. In any case, it all ends up creating a patched up job of life that may work in the short term but won't hold up for eternity.

Pray Father, I am sorry for the ways that I have tried to earn my own salvation through works. Help me not look to my own strength but accept the forgiveness you freely offer.

Reflect How have I fallen into the performance trap?

Day Ninety Two

Garden Helper

Maya loves to help me in the garden, although I use the word 'help' very loosely in this context. When she waters the plants, Maya inevitably ends up soaking wet because she apparently needed watering as well. She digs in the dirt with her little shovel, but she flings most of it out of the garden and into the grass. She pulls the flower buds off of the plants right before they have a chance to bloom. However, the most difficult thing to teach her in the garden has been how to distinguish between weeds and plants.

She sees me constantly pulling weeds and tossing them out of the garden. She also sees me planting flowers in the ground, taking care that each is placed in the best environment to thrive. Not seeing the difference between the two, she tends to go around pulling up flowers out the ground and throwing them in the grass. She also likes to gather up the weeds I have pulled and plant them back in the dirt with careful attention. I try to help her see the difference between the plants we want in the garden and those that we don't. So far, it doesn't seem to be helping.

Read

But the wisdom that comes from heaven is first of all pure; then peace-loving, considerate, submissive, full of mercy and good fruit, impartial and sincere. Peacemakers who sow in peace reap a harvest of righteousness.

—*James 3:17–18 NIV*

Apply   In the same way that Maya needs to learn to distinguish between which plants to grow and which to throw, we must be very careful about the character traits and attitudes that we allow to take root in our lives. We will know what to continue cultivating in our lives based on the fruit. If an activity, relationship, or attitude results in a life that is pure, peacemaking, considerate, submissive, merciful, impartial, and sincere, then we are on the right track.

In the same way, other activities and relationships growing in our lives can cause the opposite fruit to develop—strife, self-promotion, judgmentalism, prejudice, impurity, and falsehood. When these attitudes are present, we can be sure that there are weeds of foolishness rampant in the garden of our hearts. We must be diligent to pull out anything that could grow into these negative attitudes. We will reap what we sow!

Pray   Father, show me any attitudes, relationships, or activities that are producing negative fruits in my life and give me the initiative to pull them out. Help me to lead a life full of your wisdom.

Reflect   What weeds do I need to pull out of my life?

_____

_____

_____

_____

_____

Spitting Up

Everly is a big spit-upper. I'm not sure what causes some babies to have more spit up than others. What I do know, is that Everly always seems to do it at the most inopportune moments. I will be looking down at my beautiful baby, in complete awe at how amazing she is, when she suddenly has a stream of white spit up gush down her front. I may be showing her off to a friend at church, describing all of her wonderful qualities, when she spews all over my friend's outfit.

Or, my personal favorite, it happens right after I finally get to take a shower (a rare occurrence as a mom of littles,) and I'm smelling so nice and clean. I pick up my sweet girl only to be promptly covered in a slimy layer of spit up. I can't help but stare at my little baby and wonder how someone so adorable and lovely can expel such revolting liquids. I love her anyway!

Read

The teachers of the law and the Pharisees brought in a woman caught in adultery. They made her stand before the group and said to Jesus, "Teacher, this woman was caught in the act of adultery. In the Law Moses commanded us to stone such women. Now what do you say?" When they kept on questioning him, he straightened up and said to them, "Let any one of you who is without sin be the first to throw a stone at her."

At this, those who heard began to go away one at a time, the older ones first, until only Jesus was left, with the woman still standing there. Jesus straightened up and asked her, "Woman, where are they? Has no one condemned you?"

"No one, sir," she said.

"Then neither do I condemn you," Jesus declared. "Go now and leave your life of sin."

—John 8:3–5, 6–7, 9–11 NIV

Apply I love Everly no matter what nastiness comes out of her mouth, and Jesus exhibits unconditional love for us. Jesus has an ability to love us in spite of the ugly sin in our lives. He is not condoning the woman's sin in these verses, but rather he tells her to stop. At the same time, he does not allow her actions to taint his view of her as an individual.

This is a lesson that we struggle with as Christians. We must keep a constant balance of showing unconditional love to everyone, no matter what sin they engage in, while simultaneously continuing to view the sin as the abhorrent thing that it is. We tend to slide towards one extreme or the other. It is so easy to point to someone living in sin and condemn them rather than their actions. Likewise, it is so much easier to love someone when we simply make the sin in their lives seem less sinful than it truly is. We must use God's wisdom in order to love the sinner and hate the sin.

Pray Father, thank you for your unconditional love for me, while calling me to leave my sin behind. Allow me to show that love to others, while acknowledging the gravity of sin.

Reflect Which end of the spectrum do I tend to favor— lessening the weight of sin or my love for others?

Day Ninety Four

Prenatal Vitamins

Since I am breastfeeding Everly, I still take my prenatal vitamins, and Maya watched me take one this week.

"What's that, Mommy?"

"That is my vitamin. I take it so that my body will have everything it needs to feed Everly," I explained.

"Oh." She was eating some trail mix for a snack at the time. She carefully looked in her bowl and picked out an M&M in a color that matched my vitamins. She ate it and took a drink of water from her sippy cup just as I had from my glass. "Now I can feed Evie too!"

Read   *Hear, O Israel: The Lord our God, the Lord is one. Love the Lord your God with all your heart and with all your soul and with all your strength. These commandments that I give you today are to be on your hearts. Impress them on your children. Talk about them when you sit at home and when you walk along the road, when you lie down and when you get up. Tie them as symbols on your hands and bind them on your foreheads. Write them on the doorframes of your houses and on your gates.*

—Deuteronomy 6:4–8 NIV

Apply When breastfeeding, a mom provides all of the nourishment her baby needs, but she must make sure to be getting all of the required nutrients herself. The baby only gets what the mom herself has to give. It is the same way with a Christ-like character. We can only expect our children to act in love if we, as moms, are demonstrating it. We can only demonstrate love by taking time each day to read God's Word so that it can be incorporated into everything that we do throughout our everyday lives.

We must also make time to talk and listen to God, asking for wisdom and patience with our children and seeking his direction in even the smallest of decisions. When we have constant communion with God as an integral part of our lives, it comes through in everything that we do, from how to treat the check-out lady at the grocery store to how we handle the third toddler meltdown tantrum of the day (possibly in that same grocery store). Let's face it, we need Jesus just to get through the day!

Pray Father, thank you for equipping me to do the work that you put before me each day. I pray that you would fill me with a Christ-like character in each encounter I have today and with each interaction with my children. Allow them to see a reflection of you in the way that I treat them.

Reflect What is one way that I can allow Christ to fill me today?

Day Ninety Five

I Know My ABC's

Maya loves to sing. She sings very enthusiastically, very loudly, and very off-key. She sings in the car, in the bath, in the grocery store, and especially when I'm trying to pay a bill over the phone. Maya loves to stand on the fireplace hearth as a stage holding a spatula as a microphone and singing her little heart out!

One of Maya's favorite songs is the ABC's. She sings most of it very well, but there are a few places that she has inserted her own adaptations. She always sings, "F, E, G" instead of, "E, F, G." Another of her alterations is to say, "double X" instead of, "W, X." My favorite of her personal interpretations is instead of saying, "T, U, V," she sings, "to Evie." I love that she dedicates the song to her baby sister! Overall, she does pretty well for a two year old, but she can't keep singing it this way when she gets to Kindergarten.

Read *"And now, O Israel, listen to the statutes and the rules that I am teaching you, and do them, that you may live, and go in and take possession of the land that the Lord, the God of your fathers, is giving you. You shall not add to the word that I command you, nor take from it, that you may keep the commandments of the Lord your God that I command you.*

—Deuteronomy 4:1–2 NIV

Apply As Christians, knowing the teachings of the Bible is as basic and necessary as knowing the ABC's. Unfortunately, we are surrounded by teachings with lots of variations that do not ring true when compared with actual scripture. The only way for us to judge which teaching is authentic is to know what the Bible says for ourselves.

Before we begin pointing fingers, we must admit that we are guilty of this practice as well. We tend to add rules which aren't actually in Scripture and to leave others out which don't suit our lifestyles. For new Christians, mistakes are inevitable, but as we continue to grow in Christ, our knowledge and maturity in handling God's Word should grow exponentially.

Like Maya, singing to her sister for no apparent reason, we sometimes have motivations that are misplaced. We may use the Word of God for our own gain with ulterior motives or without the good of others in mind. Twisting the words of Scripture to fit our own wants and needs is not to be taken lightly. The words in the Bible are sacred, handed down to us from God himself, and we must handle them with the utmost respect by presenting them authentically to others.

Pray Father, thank you for the Bible, your very words and commands for me. Help me to interpret the Bible correctly, to present it authentically, and to adopt it as a whole to guide my life.

Reflect How have I given God's Word my own alterations?

Here Comes the Hulk

Maya was asked to walk in the wedding of my brother-in-law and sister-in-law. It was a beautiful ceremony with every detail thoughtfully dreamed, carefully planned, and perfectly executed. Having a toddler in a wedding is always a risk, but we had a plan. I would be at the front with Everly (less than a month old at the time) so that Maya could walk down the aisle to me. The only problem was that Nathan couldn't be at the back of the church to send her down the aisle to me, because he was playing guitar on stage for the wedding march. It would be fine, right?

I was waiting with my cell phone ready to capture the moment Maya stepped through the doors in her sweet tulle dress. We had her looking truly adorable. The bride's and groom's dogs were walking right before Maya, and she wanted to pet them, but had to wait for her turn to walk. She was not happy about that.

When her turn came, she burst through the doors raging like the Hulk. I dropped my phone. She wailed, stomped, and flailed down the entire length of the aisle looking like she would devour anyone who tried to interfere with her walk of terror. It didn't help that she was also sporting a black eye from her fall off the counter the week before. I wanted to sink into the floor and disappear.

Read

"In your anger do not sin": Do not let the sun go down while you are still angry, and do not give the devil a foothold.

—Ephesians 4:26–27 NIV

Apply

We all have moments of anger. Sometimes we wish we could rage with the unrestrained exuberance of a toddler, but that would be more than a little awkward. In these verses, Paul doesn't tell us to not get angry. Getting angry is a natural reaction and in some situations, a justified one. The important lesson to remember is to not let our anger lead us to sin.

We must find strategies to release our anger in a healthy way. The Bible teaches that the best way to relieve anger is through reconciliation, which is usually the last thing we want to do. These verses teach us to reconcile promptly, though we usually try to delay it as long as possible. When we leave time between anger and reconciliation, we give Satan room to wreak havoc like the Hulk!

Pray

Father, I'm sorry for the times that I have sinned in anger. Help me to seek reconciliation as quickly as possible. I can only do it through your strength!

Reflect

How has anger led me to sin? Who do I need to reconcile with?

_____

_____

_____

Twirly Dress

Maya loves a twirly dress. She will pick one out of her closet and say, "Mommy, I wear this one! It's so beautiful!" I will help her put it on, and she runs to my room so that she can stand on the bed and look at her reflection in the mirror. She will smile at herself and giggle. She puts on all the airs as she struts around on the bed.

Then, of course, there is lots of jumping, because it's fun to watch the dress puff up in the air on the way down. Then she starts spinning around, because watching it twirl is the best! If the dress is sparkly and catches the light, it's even better. She doesn't have to say what she is thinking out loud because it is clearly written all over her face—she is beautiful, and she is loved! She couldn't be more right!

Read

You shall be a crown of beauty in the hand of the Lord, and a royal diadem in the hand of your God. You shall no more be termed Forsaken, and your land shall no more be termed Desolate, but you shall be called My Delight Is in Her, and your land Married; for the Lord delights in you, and your land shall be married. For as a young man marries a young woman, so shall your sons marry you, and as the bridegroom rejoices over the bride, so shall your God rejoice over you.

—Isaiah 62:3–5 NIV

Apply I'm not sure where Maya learned to gape at herself in the mirror. I am lucky if I look in a mirror more than three minutes a day. As moms, we don't get a lot of free time to make ourselves look attractive, and most of the time we don't feel pretty. It is difficult to feel beautiful when we are rocking the messy bun, big t-shirt, complete with spit up on the shoulder, and post-partum leggings. Let's face it, life has changed a lot since these sweet babies arrived.

As unlovely as we may feel, these verses make it clear how God sees us. He sees us as beautiful, and he delights greatly in us! When God looks at us, he sees us as beautiful as a bride on her wedding day—the hair, the makeup, the dress, and most importantly, the contagious glow of a woman who is confident in being completely loved. God is committed to us more than any earthly husband ever could be!

Pray Father, thank you for seeing me as beautiful, valuable, and desirable. Help me to remember this when I am tempted to think differently. Let me live each day in joy with this truth hidden in my heart.

Reflect How does it make me feel to know that God rejoices over me?

_____

_____

_____

Fighting Sleep

When Maya was a baby she was extremely skilled at fighting sleep. She would be so tired but would simply refuse to close her eyes and let her body relax enough to drift off to sleep. Nathan and I devised a few methods that we found useful.

The most effective method was feeding her to sleep. Every night until she was almost seven months old, Maya would breastfeed for an hour or more until she was so full she would conk out while still latched. Another good method was movement. Most babies like to be rocked or bounced, but Maya needed much more extreme motion in order to be lulled to sleep. I would hold her and bounce on a yoga ball until she was jostled into unconsciousness.

The final method was to let her wear herself out. This always worked eventually, but would require a long time before taking effect. I would let her play on the floor or in her crib until she eventually ran out of the energy to keep her eyes open. However, I usually ran out of energy before she did!

Read *Do not conform to the pattern of this world, but be transformed by the renewing of your mind. Then you will be able to test and approve what God's will is—his good, pleasing and perfect will.*

—Romans 12:2 NIV

Apply We have been awakened to new life with Christ, but Satan has a handful of methods that he uses in an attempt to lull us out of commitment to Christ and into a spiritual slumber. He tries to feed us to sleep, indulging our desire for things and filling our appetites with temporary treasures until we are so full that we slip out of service.

Another of Satan's methods for luring us into unconsciousness in our Christian walk is movement. If He can keep us moving, busily bouncing from one good task to another, we never leave any time to realize that we have lost touch with the Savior. He can use the need for constant motion to make us conform to the world around us and lose sight of eternity. Satan's final method is letting us wear ourselves out, encouraging us to reach for perfection at an unsustainable rate. He runs the risk of our fervor for Christ outlasting his deadline, so it is not the preferred method.

In this life, God has a good, pleasing, and perfect will for us. But in order to accomplish it, we have to fight the urge to sleep spiritually, to conform to the thought patterns around us, and to live with the same set of priorities as the world. Only by being continually renewed can we effectively fight Satan's methods.

Pray Father, thank you for having a good plan for my life! Help me to fight the urge to conform to the world so that I can know and live out your will for my life.

Reflect Which of Satan's methods am I most susceptible to in conforming to the world?

Day Ninety Nine

Oatmeal Rations

I believe I have mentioned several times how Maya eats like a caveman (and I'm not talking Paleo.) She is the messiest eater in the world, and all of her favorite foods seem to have the greatest potential for being disastrous. For example, she will eat an entire adult serving of oatmeal for breakfast, but I would have to be crazy to give it to her all at once.

A full bowl of oatmeal quickly becomes a bowl of oatmeal dumped on the floor, poured in her hair, or spread across the table like finger paint—the possibilities are endless and simply too appealing for her to resist. Instead, when we eat oatmeal, I give her a small bowl with no more than four bites in it. After she eats it all, she can have four more bites worth. This rationing system has redeemed the merits of oatmeal as a breakfast food in my mind.

Read

"For it will be like a man going on a journey, who called his servants and entrusted to them his property. To one he gave five talents, to another two, to another one, to each according to his ability. Then he went away. Now after a long time the master of those servants came and settled accounts with them. And he who had received the five talents came forward, bringing five talents more, saying, 'Master, you delivered to me five talents; here, I have made five talents more.' His master said to him, 'Well done, good and faithful servant. You have been faithful over a little; I will set you over

much. Enter into the joy of your master.' And he also who had the two talents came forward, saying, 'Master, you delivered to me two talents; here, I have made two talents more.' His master said to him, 'Well done, good and faithful servant. You have been faithful over a little; I will set you over much. Enter into the joy of your master.' He also who had received the one talent came forward, saying, 'I was afraid, and I went and hid your talent in the ground. Here, you have what is yours.' But his master answered him, 'You wicked and slothful servant! Take the talent from him and give it to him who has the ten talents.'

—Matthew 25:14–15, 19–24a, 25–26a, 28 NIV

Apply I was always a bit confused by this parable until I started thinking about it in terms of oatmeal rationing. I thought it was unfair that the one with ten should get another one and that the servant with one only got one. I know how much oatmeal Maya is capable of handling at one time, and God knows how much to hold us accountable for as well.

We tend to fall into a unique trap, though. The majority of us don't fit into the category of the five-talent servant or the one-talent servant, but the two-talent servant. This gives us three options for action: we can, 1) ask God why we didn't get five talents and let jealousy cloud our own responsibility, 2) look down on the servant with one talent and let pride inhibit our perspective of responsibility, or 3) focus on the two talents that God has entrusted to us and invest them well for his kingdom. This parable is not about comparison, but about doing all we can with what we are given!

Pray Father, thank you for blessing me in so many ways and help me to use it to serve you greatly!

Reflect Who do I tend to compare myself to?

Day One Hundred

How to Eat Vegetables

Maya loves vegetables, especially green ones. Broccoli, green beans, and peas are all at the top of her favorites list. Unfortunately, she is two, therefore she must follow toddler code which calls for tantrums any time green vegetables are served. Not to worry, I decided to use another bit of toddler code to my advantage.

This code states that the toddler must attempt to eat anything on the parent's plate whether or not they like it and regardless of the fact that it may be the exact same food as on their own plate. I started serving myself vegetables at meals, but not putting any on her plate. Immediately, she wanted to eat them all. Last night, she grabbed a bunch of broccoli from my plate and started devouring it.

Then, thoughtful girl she is, Maya looked at me sweetly and asked, "You want some, Mommy? I share with you." She held out a small piece of broccoli to me. It was all I could do not to laugh out loud. Had she truly forgotten that it was actually my broccoli that she was eating? She considered herself very generous for giving back a small piece of my own broccoli that she had taken from my plate. I didn't mind—the broccoli was meant for her all along.

Read

"Will a mere mortal rob God? Yet you rob me. "But you ask, 'How are we robbing you?' "In tithes and offerings. You are

under a curse—your whole nation—because you are robbing me. Bring the whole tithe into the storehouse, that there may be food in my house. Test me in this," says the LORD Almighty, "and see if I will not throw open the floodgates of heaven and pour out so much blessing that there will not be room enough to store it. "Then all the nations will call you blessed, for yours will be a delightful land," says the LORD Almighty.

—*Malachi 3:8–10, 12 NIV*

Apply   In the same way that I set aside the broccoli for Maya to eat, God has blessings in store for us. He has promised to provide for our needs, and he is faithful. Yet we seem unable to grasp that these blessings were not ours to begin with. We quickly accept gifts from God and claim them as our own to use for our own pleasure and fulfillment. Throughout the Bible, God calls us to give back to him from what he has given to us.

Just as Maya's small token of shared broccoli warmed my heart, God looks at our gifts back to him as small in his grand scheme, and yet generous, as we give out of gratitude. When we fail to give back, we are taking what isn't ours and using it for a purpose it was not intended for. God will not continue to bless those who live in ungrateful greed, but is willing to lavishly provide for those who are generous with what he has given them. When we remember where our blessings have originated, it is easy to share with others.

Pray   Father, thank you for promising to provide for me. Help me remember that these blessings come from you and to give joyfully and generously back to you.

Reflect   In what ways have I robbed God, taking his blessings without sharing them with others for his glory?

A Note from the Author

I am truly honored that you traveled through the last one hundred days sharing these learnable moments with me. While the devotional is finished, your journey with learnable moments is just beginning! You see, learnable moments are all around you! God is trying to teach you about himself every day in small ways. I hope that this journey has helped you to create a habit of recognizing the learnable moments in your own life.

As we part ways, I would love to give you two challenges. The first challenge is to be intentional in looking for learnable moments in your everyday life. The second is for you to write them down so that you can remember the many ways that God has provided for you and the lessons he has taught you. Trust me, these moments, if remembered, will serve you well over and over again.

I would love to stay connected with you! Drop by our website for helpful blog posts for moms as well as new books and products. If you want to share your learnable moments with me, I would love to read them! You can share them through the 'contact us' page of the website. Thaks again for taking on the challenge of giving God your attention throughout our devotions together!

God Bless,
Erin Greneaux

greneauxgardens.com